A Shadow's Cry

A Collected Omnibus

Consisting of Dark Poetry from a Troubled Mind,
The Fires of Judgment, Ballads of Lost Lenoria, and
The Song of the Vampire

By Anthony Uyl MTS

Devoted Publishing
Ingersoll, Ontario. Canada 2023

A Shadow's Cry
A Collected Omnibus
Consisting of Dark Poetry from a Troubled Mind, The Fires of Judgment, Ballads of Lost Lenoria, and The Song of the Vampire
By Anthony Uyl MTS

Cover and Paper Background designs done by Zsuzsa Fige and are the property of 2165467 Ontario Inc.

ISBN: 978-1-77356-435-7

The text of A Shadow's Cry is all protected under Copyright ©2023 Devoted Publishing. The covers, background, layout, and Devoted Publishing logo are Copyright ©2023 Devoted Publishing. This edition is published by Devoted Publishing a division of 2165467 Ontario Inc.

Unless written permission is given for any original material, all use of this material to be reproduced, stored in a retrieval system, or transmitted in any form by any means, electronic, mechanical, photocopying, recording or otherwise is forbidden. All rights reserved.

Contact Us Online:
Email: office@devotedpub.com
Facebook: @devotedpublishing
Authors' Twitter: @AnthonyUyl
For more information on Biblical Demonology and issues with the occult in modern evangelicalism, check out the authors' Substack Blog Reformed Demonology: reformeddemonology.substack.com

Table of Contents

Preface 11
A Shadow's Cry 13
   1. Demon Man 13
   2. 14
   3. A Savior Comes 15
   4. 16
   5. The Warriors Song 17
   6. The Bandit 18
   7. The Fox 19
   8. Deimos 20
   9. Stalker 21
   10. The Warrior 25
   11. The Destroyer 26
   12. 27
   13. Blind Evil 28
   14. Alive 29
   15. 30
   16. 31
   17. Jihad 32
   18. The Third Brother 33
   19. 34
   20. Counterstrike 35
   21. The Battlefield 36
   22. Nothing 37
   23. 38
   24. And I Cried 39
   25. 40
   26. The Stalker Reborn ... 41
   27. Darkness Reigns 42
   28. Hail the Leader 43
   29. 44
   30. Breath from Heaven . 45
   31. 46
   32. The Wolf 47
   33. The Phoenix 48
   34. The Stalker Comes ... 49
   35. Shadows 50
   36. Sickness 51
   37. Kingdom 52
   38. Secrets 53
   39. Beneath the Mask 54
   40. Beauty and the Shadow 55
   41. Stalker's Praise 56
   42. 57
   43. 58
   44. Torture 59
   45. 60
   46. Stalker Again 61
   47. Control 62
   48. 63
   49. Were-Wolf 64
   50. 65
   51. Tell Me 66
   52. Faith 67
   53. I Came Back 68
   54. Where Am I Going Now? 69
   55. 70

56. 71	85. 103
57. Tomorrow 72	86. Call Out 104
58. 74	87. Freak 105
59. Bondage 75	88. Puppy 106
60. 76	89. War 107
61. 77	90. Alive? 108
62. 78	91. Bride of Cain 109
63. 79	92. Child of Blood 110
64. Reject 80	93. Rainfall 111
65. 82	94. Cry of the Earth 112
66. Fuel, Blood and Water 83	95. Here I Wait 113
67. Tower 84	96. Heretics 114
68. 85	97. Ascension 115
69. Uneasy Peace 86	98. The Prisoner 116
70. Love Song of the Unforgiven 87	99. 117
71. 89	100. Power Lie 118
72. 90	101. The Fence 119
73. Part of Me 91	102. Get A Life 121
74. Why 92	103. Destiny 122
75. 93	104. The Avengement .. 123
76. Youth 94	105. Let Me Fly 124
77. 95	106. Confession 125
78. 96	107. Imperial March 126
79. 97	108. Living Nightmare . 128
80. 98	109. Dream Angel 129
81. 99	110. No Matter 130
82. 100	111. Dance With Me 131
83. 101	112. Oppress 132
84. 102	113. Cry 133
	114. I am Free 134

115. 135	144. 165
116. Alone 136	145. 166
117. I Stand 137	146. 167
118. Angel of Mine 138	147. 168
119. Mother Earth 139	148. 169
120. 140	149. 171
121. Fantasy World 141	150. 172
122. What Dreams May Come 142	151. 173
	152. 174
123. Lemmings 143	153. 175
124. 144	154. 176
125. Dark Lord 145	155. Can Not Feel 177
126. 146	156. Beat Me 178
127. 147	157. The Prayer 179
128. 148	158. Curse 180
129. 149	159. The Damned 181
130. 150	160. Thief 182
131. 151	161. 183
132. 152	162. 184
133. 153	163. 185
134. Star 154	164. 186
135. 155	165. 188
136. Freedom 156	166. 189
137. 157	167. 190
138. 158	168. 191
139. 159	169. 192
140. 160	170. 193
141. 162	171. 194
142. 163	172. 195
143. 164	173. 197

174.	198
175.	199
176.	200
177. Dead	201
178.	202
179.	204
180. Blue Cheese	206
181.	207
182. Vampyre	208
183. Dark Angelica	209
184.	211
185.	212
186.	213
187. Seraph	214
188.	215
189.	216
190.	217
191.	218
192.	219
193.	220
194.	221
195. My Gift to You	224
196.	226
197.	227
198.	228
199.	229
200.	230
201.	231
202.	232
203.	233
204.	234
205.	235
206.	236
207.	238
208.	239
209.	240
210.	241
211.	242
212.	244
213.	245
214.	247
215.	248
216.	249
217.	250
218.	251
219.	252
220. Love Song of the Unforgiven II	253
221.	255
222.	257
223.	260
224.	262
225.	263
226.	267
227.	268
228.	269
229. The Escape	271
230. The Black Widow	273
231. Wasted Life	275
232. Homefront	277

233.	279
234.	281
235.	282
236.	283
237. Mommy and Daddy	284
238. The Family	285
239.	287
240.	288
241.	289
242.	291
243.	292
244.	294
245.	295
246.	296
247.	297
248.	298
249.	300
250.	301
251.	302
252.	303
253.	304
254.	305
255.	306
256. God's Rose	307
257. Catalyst	309
258. My Prayer for You	310
259. Play God	311
260. Undead	312
261.	314
262.	316
263.	317
264. Bloodroses	318
265.	321
266.	322
267.	323
268.	324
269.	325
270.	326
271.	327
272.	328
273.	329
274.	330
275.	331
276.	334
277.	335
278.	336
279.	337
280.	338
281.	339
282.	340
283.	342
284.	343
285.	344
286.	345
287.	346
288.	347
289.	348
290.	349
291.	350

292. 351
293. 352
294. 353
295. 354
296. 355

A Shadow's Cry: The Fires of Judgment 356

  Chapter 1: The Illusion. 356

    1. 356
    2. 357
    3. Birth of a Star 358
    4. Dark Wood 359
    5. Jewels of Night 360
    6. Luna 361
    7. Symphony 362
    8. The Tower 363
    9. Tree-King 364

  Chapter 2: The Reality . 365

    10. 365
    11. 366
    12. 367
    13. 368
    14. 369
    15. 370
    16. 371
    17. 372
    18. 373
    19. 374
    20. 375
    21. 376

22. 377
23. 378
24. 379
25. 380
26. 381
27. 382
28. 383
29. 384
30. 385
31. 386
32. 387
33. 388
34. 389
35. 390
36. 391
37. 392
38. 393
39. 394
40. 395
41. 396
42. 397
43. 398
44. Blood Drips 399
45. Daughter Nation . 400
46. Detestable Things 401
47. Forgotten Stable . 404
48. Freedom 405
49. Our Example 406
50. Poltergeist 407
51. Right Road 408

52. Salvation 410
53. Self-Help 411
54. Tears 413
55. The Curtain 414
56. The Door 415
57. The Tempter 416

Chapter 3: The Judgment
.... 417

58. Prophet of the End
.... 417
59. 419
60. 420
61. 421
62. 422
63. 423
64. 424
65. 425
66. 426
67. 427
68. 428
69. 429
70. 430
71. 431
72. 432
73. 433
74. 434
75. 435
76. 436
77. 437
78. Lament Against Parliament 438
79. Lost Glory 439
80. Sulphur 440
81. The Irishman 441

Chapter 4: The Hope 442

82. 442
83. 443
84. 444
85. 445
86. 446
87. 447
88. 448
89. 449
90. 450
91. 451
92. 452
93. 453
94. 454
95. 455
96. 456
97. 457
98. 458
99. 459
100. 460
101. 461
102. 462
103. Not Be Conquered
.... 463
104. Rising Hope 464
105. Sparrows 465
106. The Image 466

Ballads of Lost Lenoria: A Shadow's Cry Anthology. 467

    Introduction 467

    Lost Lenoria 468

    The Elf Maid 469

    Dark Rider Hunting 471

    Dwarf King 472

    Awaiting the Dawn 473

    Hunt Some Orc 474

    The Elven Queen 475

    The Necromancer 476

    The Red Dragon 477

    Mountain Caretakers 478

    Giant Tyrants 479

    An Adventure 480

    Forest for the Trees 481

    Evil Wizard 482

    Fortress of Heaven 483

    Orc Lord 484

    Elven Lord 485

    Dead Armies 486

    The Mountain Pass 487

    The Drow Princess 488

    White Wolf 489

    Southern Jungles 490

    Temple Lords 491

    The Paladin 492

    Knights of Sanctity 493

    Wrath of War 494

    Purifying Fire 495

    The Ancient River 496

    The Great Sea 497

    Charron's Herald 498

    Glade of the Druids 499

    Nymph Queen 500

    Tower of Night 501

    Temptations of Gold 502

    The Guild 503

    Robed Pilgrim 504

    Tavern Tales 505

    Forgotten Places 506

    Bard's Song 507

A Shadow's Cry: The Song of the Vampire 508

    Introduction 508

    Dead and Sunshine 509

    Skin and Dreams 510

    Dead Desires 511

    Forever Lost 512

    Memories 513

    The Beast in Me 514

    The Prey 515

    Death Penalty 516

    Damnation 517

    Truth and Darkness 518

    Take My Life 519

    Red Thirst 520

    History is a Lie 521

    Your Fragrance 522

    A Calling 523

Power of Will 524	Mortal Hunters.............. 537
Shall I Create 525	Judgment Comes 538
Unchangeable 526	Moonfaced 539
The Craving 527	Crypt Sleeper 540
Evil 528	The Roamer 541
Other Malevolents 529	A Pit of Sheol 542
The Wolf 530	Eternal Curse 543
Hidden Thoughts 531	Assassins 544
Cult of the Shade 532	Mortal Evil.................... 545
Immortal Insanity 533	The Meeting Point 546
Sounds of the City 534	Nothing Left for Us 547
Burning Light 535	Lord of the Dead........... 548
Fog at Midnight............ 536	

Preface

When I originally published these volumes, I wasn't the most experienced publisher in the world. Nor was I the most experienced writer in the world either. There were multiple spelling and grammatical mistakes that at the time of original publishing, I didn't care about.

As time went on and I looked at these books, the grammar in them continued to bother me. While the print options at the time were limited, since print-on-demand options have largely expanded, it made sense to go back through all four books, fix what mistakes I could find and then republish them. This means that there could be mistakes still and if there are, I do sincerely apologize!

There were other issues as well. The big one was the foul language that I was using in the first of these four volumes. While I wasn't as mature as I am now and my mental health issues made this a non-issue for me, as the years have gone on, again, God has convicted me that this needed to change. The time has finally come that I put that conviction to work and change the language. While I have gone over the original book, there may still be some terms that people will find objectionable. I tried my best to search them out and if I missed one, again, this wasn't on purpose. I hope that you don't take any offense where none was meant.

One final issue I wanted to address was a theological one. While at the time of writing some of this poetry I believed that referring to God as "Daddy" would make the poetry more personal, with the emergence of the Word-of-Faith movement using this terminology and also hyper-charismatics, I decided that this is an openly blasphemous way to talk about our heavenly and holy God. So, when the term "daddy' was being using in reference to the holy God the Father, it was removed and replaced with the obvious word, "father." While this has removed some of the elegance of the poems as they were originally written, I could not excuse my conscience and ignore the issue. Anyone who knows me well enough will know that a theological problem in my own writing will bother me until the world's end. And I couldn't allow that to remain in a work of this magnitude.

What I am hoping for, is that those that struggle with mental health issues, as I have for my entire life, can find a peace in the comfort that is our God. While many in churches around the world will speak without authority on the issue, many are trying to help. We need to show them some grace on this issue. Mental health from a biblical standpoint, is because of the invasion of sin on God's world. However, it does not mean that because you struggle with anxiety that it is because you have wilfully done something wrong and need to repent. Our bodies, having been affected by an evil invasion, have physically had to deal with parts of our bodies that simply do not want to work properly. For those dealing with mental health, this can be an issue. I have had many Christians over the years try to tell me that if I would just "be happy, it'll all go away." For those who think this, that is like telling someone that has no legs, to just get up and start walking. It doesn't work that way and we all need to show a bit of grace to those that suffer with problems that we simply don't have the expertise to speak on.

At the same time, many "mental health" issues that are being claimed in doctor's offices, are simply people trying to find a quick and easy way to deal with problems they have either caused themselves or had happen to them. In a majority of these cases, it is not an issue you need medication for, it is something you need biblical counselling to deal with. The issue of mental health has never been a "one cure solves all" issue. Yet for many in the Christian world and in the secular world, they have treated it as such. Everyone needs to stop doing this. People are suffering and giving a quick "I know everything about this when I actually don't" diagnosis to theirr friends and people online, which is not helping the way they think it is. If anything, it is both emotionally and spiritually abusive.

One note about the first of the four volumes in this omnibus. When I was in high school in the late nineties, someone I had a schoolyard crush on accused me of stalking her. When I was that age, I was awkward and had a very difficult time talking to women. I still do today, to a point. It wasn't until my early twenties, in the early 2,000's, that I finally realized that if I don't go up and talk to these girls, I will never find the companionship, or God helper I am searching for. As a result, my awkward attempts to talk to this girl led her to believe I was stalking her, when I wasn't. Many years of emotional abuse from others in my high school followed. No one wanted to listen to my side of the story and at times I was physically assaulted while minding my own business.

I wish I could go back and change what happened, but it is too late for that. Bullying will never go away. Law makers can legislate anti-bullying laws and regulations all they want, but kids, even teenagers do not care. All young people are really like dogs that will go after and attack what they consider an "inferior" canine to make themselves look better and find a higher place in "the pack." It's a brutal analogy, but it is unfortunately true.

Parents need to do better when raising their children and the current generation of young parents are either the bullies or the bullied and are teaching their kids not to put up with that behaviour and the bullying circles are continuing. There needs to be another way. I believe that a biblical approach to the issue is needed, but many will simply not want to accept that as viable.

I hope this massive volume is a source of comfort, hope and a voice that helps you to see that you are not alone in this world. Many people are suffering with mental health problems. It is not appropriate that we celebrate them and parade them around, but we need to be treating these people with the love of Christ that they need to get the help that is required.

- Anthony Uyl
Owner/President of Devoted Publishing and the Author of these books.

A Shadow's Cry

1. Demon Man

Slowly the veil of darkness falls
The ghostly sound of the coyote's howl
And the mystery of the evening wind
Becomes the solemn key
An awakened soul leaps out from its resting shell
And hunts till the presence of dawn
It hunts, terrorizes and slays its prey
To feed its blood thirsty soul
Who is this man that stalks the night?
Who is this man that frightens the inner child?
He is a creature of darkness
A token of hate
Created by the years of fear and rage
By the years of his tearful scorn
He sees without seeing
He hunts without hunting
He's here and yet he's there
He is the demon man
He is the curse
He was an agent of love
He cared for all around him
Yet by love he sought
And by love he fell
His fall from grace destroyed his soul
And now he shall not love again
Why now does he fear the light?
His truth so clouded by that of which he was
Now his passion for hatred has slain him
But yet his wounds have not hurt him
(A light has reached the angel within)
Who is this demon man?
(Who is this new love he has found?)
Who will set him free?

2.

When the weight of the world
Is on your shoulders
And your dreams have been wisped away
Emotion has no purpose
And people have no face
My body is just a shell
Without you no purpose exists
And the weight of this world
Kills my soul

I would hand my heart to you
And let your beauty gleam
But the worlds twisted evil
Has blackened my soul

I have loved yet once
And may never love again
Slain by the dagger of injustice
I walk with an open wound
Bleeding as a river flows
I dare not wonder where it goes
Heal my wounds and let me know love
For you have a power over me
That I do not understand

Revenge has become my ally
I will avenge my soul's destruction
I will leap out of the darkness
I can slay the injustice
I will do this to protect you
For if they knew my love for thee
The injustice would come to slay
I would rather be slain twice
Then let you receive damnation

3. A Savior Comes

When darkness falls
With the veil of night
It ushers in a time of fright
Unknown to the naked eye
The demon men pass by and by
Fearing only that which we can perceive
Every day we live is Hallows eve
Cursing I am to their final breath
Their voice brings in cold and death
Why then do we fear them?
Why then do we not see
When will their reign of terror end?
When then will He a Savior send?
But low behold a Savior comes
In the hearts and voices of His peoples tongue
At their command they flee in fright
Away from even holy sight
Who are these ones a Savior keeps
That he proceeds to fight these hellish freaks
They are the chosen, who do not fear
Because they know
That even now
That a Savior comes

4.

A lonely heart
A wandering soul
A ghostly creep
As spirits in tales untold
Broken dreams
And bleeding wounds
Crying out
To an empty room
Echoing forth
Into this night
Despair and hope
From pain and love
Solely traveling
Through these days
Long he journeys
To far away
Escaping death
That growling ghoul
He leaps yet forth
To desperate ruin
A soul as hard as these brick walls
The harder you hit
The harder you'll fall
Screaming forth
To days ahead
He comes yet back
A lonely heart
A wondering soul
Where is his peace
Who knows?
Who knows?

5. *The Warriors Song*
Crying out the warrior's song
We will battle all this night long
Although foul foes and creatures come
Their screams of pain to us in rum
Our companion sword we bear as arms
Protecting our cities towns and farms
Frenzied like some crazed animal
We'll use what weapons we've got in our arsenal
Be it from fingers and teeth to gouge
To a blade for heads to be dislodged
'Bring it on' we cry aloud
Our courage to them is a frightful sound
Slicing the head of some poor wench
We will stick the trophy on our fence
Blackening the battlefield with blood
And like oozing soup the rivers flood
Blood lust overtaking our sweat filled eyes
We'll with honor fight where the standard flies
Surrender is not a song we sing
But their defeat is what we'll bring
And when the bitter fighting ends
We'll mourn our fallen their honor to defend
Sparing the women and children to live
May they forgive us for what we did
And as the soldiers look into the sky
Drunk and singing from the rum and rye
They sing one last song
Their voices resounding like a mighty gong
Victory is life
Life is war
And death ...
Is the only true ...
Peace

6. The Bandit

The clever bandit masked as night
Never is to doubt its might
It will pry its way into any spot
Only sometimes it will be caught
When it is it will fight with courage
To keep what it got when it rummaged
If loses or not it will be back
So be prepared and do not slack
Or it'll get you again
And again ...
And again ...
And again ...

7. The Fox

Cunning, sly and mischievous
Not caring about these ones of us
It takes what it wants with ruthless glee
Then vanishing gone before you see
Taking advantage of your work
It pays you back like a real pain
Leaving you with a mess to clean
Its cuteness makes it unseen
It's the fox
We'll get you
One of these days

8. Deimos

It creeps on you so cautious so slow
Being part of the going flow
So, it causes fear does it seem
Yet much darker and bleaker does it gleam
It causes you to remain awake
Your concrete walls it can shake
Leaving your lights on at night
Is a symbol of its awesome might
Never wanting to be alone
Is another one of its war song drones
Avoiding your enemies everyday
Will cause your ropes to forever fray
But when you decide to face it down
Will force it down the drain to drown
And when the light suddenly goes out
No more in the darkness will you pout
Being alone you will no longer fear
The veil of darkness will start to seer
Enemies will become your friends
Problems will find sudden ends
Either it will rule, dominate your life
Or you can make it flee at its own strife
Terror
Deimos
May it never be

9. Stalker

Shadowing the night with glistening ease
Creating uncertain truths
Draping reality with denial
With a mask of lies to hide a face
Wearing a clock of enigma'd rights
Evolving terror out of basic love
Who is this mind sorrowing fiend?
Who knows?
Who knows?

The living shadow an immortal thought
A dark warrior with hopes of despair
The circle of fear in a squared out world
Element of hell to the peace of mind
Shining black star in the midst of day
Aura so dark the sunlight dies
Who is this mind sorrowing fiend?
Who knows?
Who knows?

Watching you with careless eyes
Shattering dreams with ruthless glee
Being every place at once
Joyful pain is half the fun
Creviced hope a secret lust
Your private life has been unlocked
Who is this mind sorrowing fiend?
Who knows?
Who knows?

The world that's spied on is an evil one
Yet that is ancient news
Masked in veils of shadows night
Creeping in the light of day
No creature sees his demon face
No one searches for the truths

Who is this mind sorrowing fiend?
Who knows?
Who knows?

Talons of darkness block the sun
Slumbering in a hidden place
The innocent flesh thought so dear
Has come back to claim her night
The throne of darkness claimed by him
Will not be given to such disgrace
Who is this mind sorrowing fiend?
Who knows?
Who knows?

Soup like blood floods the streets
For a victory as yet untold
Gory screams of loved pain
Echo within the stars
Angel hands clasp the demons life
As its soul gets flung down to hell
Who is this mind sorrowing fiend?
Who knows?
Who knows?

A blood-stained sun curses the vampiric earth
As the new dark queen gives demon life
Cries of pain fill the clouds
While a soul gets pulled from Hells cracks
Tormented cries cease at once
While the child hides his demon face
Who is this mind sorrowing fiend?
Who knows?
Who knows?

Battle cries wail with the wind
As the child fights for his home
The Queen mother flees from him
As he pursues in a Jihad revenge

Lightning cracks the final blood
As the vengeful demon fight tyrannical love
Who is this mind sorrowing fiend?
Who knows?
Who knows?

The temple of Heaven disgraced in hate
Is justices final judge
The hate between these two damned souls
Comes back at their God's command
The concluding blast of fiery breath
Consumes both in each other's detest
Who is this mind sorrowing fiend?
Who knows?
Who knows?

Sun rays beat on this mound of bone
Where ants rebuild their hived homes
His hollow eyes bear silent witness
On the lonely plains where he lies now
Of the fight he fought and died alone
To fight for the corrupt angel's soul
Who is this mind sorrowing fiend?
Who knows?
Who knows?

Blinding rays of darkness light
Surround this damned shell
Placing it into a fired chariot
It ascends to the stars sky
No sign is left of it who he was
To remain a shadow in everyone's mind
Who is this mind sorrowing fiend?
Who knows?
Who knows?

The heavens smile that now is done
A secret war everyone fought

For an unhero who died alone in the night
And fought for peace, yet being a demon
Yet no one ever saw his face
Only an imaginary soul
Who was this mind sorrowing fiend?
Who knew?
Who knew?

They knew
Heaven and hell knew
She knew
That he was Stalker

10. The Warrior

Gleaming warrior standing tall
Defending the home with honor
Fiery ruins left by war
Is all he stands for
Unholy blood litters his sword
From defending a barren Hades
Tired from these endless days
Will he ever get to see his home?
No, he won't
No until he dies ...
For what he lives for

11. The Destroyer

Draping your eyes with deceptive love
Rocking an imaginative world
A midnight crow overcoming a nest
Destroying your eggs to plant its own
Caring nothing about the world
Driven by hate so deep so cold
Like germs it rots your dreams
With mold it grows to control
Making your days the burning hell
Causing the pagan to cry out to God
With puppy eyes your forgiveness to give
Knowing your gullible to believe this lie
Shaking from fear you start to cry
Your screams overshadowed by its looming figure
Its' extending hand the gun of love
Then all
Goes black

12.
Hearing the sound of the soothing rain
Releases the pain of this grateful sorrow
Undetermined wrath now is gone
And uncried tears have dried away
The stirred soul rests with ease
Shivering fear has calmed in the new born mists
Then fires of courage consume the heart
And the strength of love finds your veins
But as quickly as it came now it's gone
The rain has stopped, and the sun is here
The burning fires of heat touch your soul
Rays of brilliant light touch the eyes
Your eyes then see wisdom in the light
And the suns fire burns your wall of lies
And you see…
The strength you found in love makes you weak
And the fires of courage are charring you
The mists have taken your fear to give you terror
And the stirred soul once again panics with fright
Fountaining tears warp your skin
Uncontrolled wrath consumes you
Unforgiving sorrow causes you to be alone
And you hear frightening silence

13. Blind Evil

White lies wrapped in truth
With warped denial the twisted news
Deceptive eyes and prying minds
Destroying the world and all mankind
Demons of day and angels of night
The human heart with evil bleeds
Blackened thoughts the ruling king
True evil songs our mouths do sing
Blasphemous teaching corrupting minds
Grinding souls till dust is fine
Causing fear itself to flee
Blinded eyes we cannot see

14. Alive

The golden sun woke me this morn
A new day with new pains, new sorrows
Torn from my utopian dream world
Forced to face realities lies
I just don't want to face it again
I wish life's sweet end would come

But I am still alive
Just like I promised to you
I'll continue to face life's hardships
To keep that one promise to you
Even in life's darkest hour
When all seems lost
The anchor that keeps me going
Is the promise I made to you

Fighting in life's war with pain
Mortally wounded by grief
Bleeding all my joy away
Till the sky clouds over with death
Yet no matter how bleak the day seems
I'll stay alive

In the future days that seem dark
Sitting alone forgotten by you
My dead heart will pump its life
Breathing poisoned air to live
And through the meaningless love when you're gone
I will live on

Staying alive
I'm trying to stay alive
Just for you

15.
A mystic breath by supernatural senses
Soothing an angry soul in distressed times
Seeing an aura of glory through dimmed eyes
From an angel's face in a demons age
Guided by an untouched hand
Following an endless path
The unreachable soul unnaturally unique
A righteous mind so pure so true
A hustling hive of chaotic paranoia
Merging the face of the beautiful one
A beauty so sharp to kill
A lightning dagger of innocent charm
Flowing beauty on a windless day
Magnificent cheer expressed in life's gloom
Amazing glory more than a moonlit night
Brilliant radiance dimming the sun
A white rose in a dead field
A candle in the darkest hour
A sweet note in bitter quiet
An aroma of freedom in a classroom cage

16.
I dared this road of pain
To see the beautiful face
A face that you lose your pain in,
Its aura comforts troubled souls

But your mask of lies,
Can't fool us all
I've seen your perfect soul,
And know your hidden truths.

You're nothing but a liar
An earthly demon child
I was wrong to even think,
I could love a slut like you.

17. Jihad

Dark nights and fear filled days
Drive the mind to the point it's insane
Crying out to an unlistening ear
No one cares to hear about your pain

Demon possessed people with empty eyes
Vampires feeding off your sorrow
What you think is angels light
Is someone ready to run you down

Down here living in this earth hell
Living our lives to please the world
Watching eyes, hoping we fail
So they can laugh while watching us drown

This dirty filth ruling the world
A growing mold that will destroy the earth
They don't see the world's pain
All they want is glory and fame

Yet that glory comes from your pain
They'll drink your blood, to put you in shame
Your yelps of despair, their music divine
And living their lives in their luxurious crime

Hey, you what can you say?
For most people it's the only way
For them to believe they are free
In this worlds oppression and tyranny

Why do we still use our voices to fight this war?
When all these freaking people don't care anymore
For the only music rhythm they will hear
Is for us to declare…
A holy war.

18. The Third Brother

A banner of peace goes before him
Stones of good works pave his roads
Truth and light forge his army
His stories will once again be told

But sooner than later it'll change
Peace will be a dream long forgotten
He will become much worse than the second
Auschwitz will be a resort holiday

The righteous will be carried to the butcher
Death will be an accepted fling
The night will last but forever
His Victory songs no longer will they sing

19.
Waiting on tomorrow's dream
Evading the mindless thoughts
A constant shadow blocking the sun
The reigning darkness has come

20. Counterstrike

Feel the darkness, taste the night
All this evil, seems so right
My corrupted soul, with uneased pain
The lightning booms, with acidic rain
My stabbed heart, cries aloud
The sunshine hides behind the clouds
This dark lord with unanswered sin
I'll revenge myself until le fin
My infested mind will kill the thought
Of the one I died for, the one I sought
I'll make her pay for my years of sorrow
She'll wish she didn't see tomorrow

Yet when I raise the pistol sights
And glare into her pitiful eyes
I see a peace I've never known
A calm peace where everything will be alright
How can this cursed woman melt me so?
Why does she destroy my invincible walls?
Maybe there's still that flame of hope?
Maybe just maybe

21. The Battlefield

I walked across the field of sorrow and pain
To find all my old friends slain and passed away
Eyes staring to the sky reliving their last breath
With mighty demonic slashes that stole their souls away
That's the way life throws its curves
'Till you surrender your soul to its grasp
Its evil sadistic ways will make you sick
Yet it works its will until the last
It sings its sweet illusions till we turn our back
And before you know it it's brought the end
Making you pray tomorrow will never come
Leaving you with wounds no miracle could mend
But that's the way the world works its dark magic
'Till nothings left for you to hope for
When everything else has passed away
The only thing left is you being lapped up on the shore

22. Nothing

I don't expect the world to see me
I don't expect the world to understand
Because I've lost faith in an emotion
An emotion people talk so much about
They say that it heals old wounds
They say that it crosses mountains and oceans
They say that it can end a war
They say that it is all you need
Yet it's the one that inflicted the wound
It forced me to hide in mountains and drowned me in its waves
It flung me into a war that will not end
What good is this mighty emotion of love?
All its done is turned its back
And flung my heart into the sea
Every night its demons haunt me
My mind is tortured with its thought
What has love ever done for me?
Nothing
This pointless emotion,
Has done nothing

23.
Above the sky in the good beyond
Lies a beautiful world where many aren't fond
A continuous light show day and night
Which streak and burn all time long

24. And I Cried

I sprung awake at 2 am
To find my dreams were filled with her again
As hard as I tried a tear fell forth
All I saw was her dream till morn
Yet it was a dream of despair
Where she with tyranny and fear reigned
She clutched my heart in her iron cold claws
In a dungeon I laid and drown in my own blood
Then I sat and cried
Trying to flush the pain down
And I sat and cried
In memory of a dream that never was
I tried to live out that day
Without seeing her, trying not to care
My thoughts bore her dreaded face
And I glanced in her eyes where dreams are made
Then I broke and cried
Tried to slow my heart down
And I broke and cried
While my heart beat out her name
Watched her walk by gracefully sweet
The air filled with her beautiful scent
Ignored my broken, lying corpse
And left me there to drown in my tears
But when I looked at her passing peace
She glanced back at me so eased
Looked at me with holy fire
With a twinkle in her eye
And…
I watched her cry
Filled with the same sorrow and pain
And I watched her cry
As the twinkle fell softly in my hand

25.

The crack of dawn enlightens the new day
An engine sputter's, crackles and turns
'Till the slumbered lion roars to rest
And ushers in a time of chaos
King and rulers do not oppose it
Demons fear in its quake
A twisted shot of disfate
Brings it forth into the world
A shake and rumble of impacting metal
Opens the eyes and awakes the dragon
A banshee screams as the missile fires
An arrow of hell brings a soul to its end
The patter of raining death flails
And punctures the iron skin of another
The screaming fire leaves him to bleed
Swerving in circles to and fro
Avoiding the mirror force
As hard as you try
The final shriek is all you hear
Until the man-made hell of divorcing atoms
Rocks you into silent slumber

26. The Stalker Reborn

I crawl out, from my hole of pain
I gaze out, to this world death game
I come out, from the shadows labyrinth
I stand up, to take back the night

The priests sing their songs of joy
At the return of this demon child
Summoned forth from his realms of shadows
He's here to release his reign of fear again
Who is this face that all fear
That is reborn in a princess's womb
Who is this mind sorrowing fiend?
To whom the night bows
To whom night creatures sing
And the storm obeys
He is the alpha and omega
The beginning and the end
The beginning of terror
The end of peace
He is the Stalker reborn
Reincarnated in this time of peace
To once again reign with terror
As he did once before

I rule now, from my dark throne
I conquer now, with songs of war
I destroy now, all hopes and dreams
I Stalk now, to make you shake…
In fear

27. Darkness Reigns

Feel the shiver of night itch down your spine
Know terror for injustice to this acquitted crime
Quake in the darkness as it enshrouds your soul
You try to scream in your pain, but you can't
For the darkness reigns in the light of night
This shadowed soul says it will be alright
Their tyranny has come to oppress your mind
All the peace you want now you cannot find

28. Hail the Leader

In the crypts of the starlit night
Live a race of pure ones we know to be
In the fortress courtyard we hear their cry
They honor the leader of human purity
In this age of dark infested blood
His blood of light has come through the sky
All who see his know he's the human one
They join the chorus of his name
His army marches to take back the world
And instrument his age of purity
All who stand against him will fall to dust
As he becomes leader of a new hierarchy
When the smoke of war thins right out
All will see him for his royalty
The age of light, will reign supreme
All the people will cry out his name

29.

As I take these few steps
To the angel within you
I feel like I'm taking a journey
I'm fated to complete
The warrior that was in me
Was wounded under the pressure
But beaten he limped to you
Then we danced upon the stars
And when I looked into your eyes
The storms of fear did dissipate
And the dreams in my mind
Were as real as you to me
I couldn't help but let out a tear
I knew you were the one I cared
A fantasy I could never have hoped for
Had just been fulfilled that night
Then you had to go, and it hurt
That this fantasy would end suddenly
I couldn't look back for the fear I'd cry
And that you wouldn't return

30. Breath from Heaven

I walk down life's way
And see the marvel of creation
The trees bristling
And the creek trickling
As the night creeps up
I see the stars above
Alone there with tear filled eyes
I whisper out your name
You must be a breath from heaven
For the angels bowed
And the stars burned with brighter fire
The man in the moon smiled as a tear fell
As the wind carried your name through rustling trees
And then I knew at that moment
You are ...
A breath from heaven

31.

Who's gonna be there when you cry
Who's gonna hug you when you say farewell
Who's gonna be there when your heart shutters to the wind
Who's gonna be there when you die
Happily, it won't be me
I'll shove this hose right up your butt
To help you cry through the night
And I won't give you one once of pity

32. The Wolf

The shadowed beast that haunts the wood
None approach for fear of retaliation
In the cold of day, it is seen
But its quiet mystery is all you see
Yet when night comes its stalking howl
You hear, but you can't see
This ghostly form seems small, unthreatening
But in truth, it's strength …
Can send the moose crashing to its knees
And send the bear away in fright
This small, stalking predator dog
Wolf, what other mysteries do you hold?

33. The Phoenix

The night flares to life in its presence
Consumed in fire in living life
All can see this beautiful sight
None can doubt that
This bird of fire sings to the stars
Souls are calmed by this tune
Soar high Phoenix one
Let the world see

34. The Stalker Comes

Wrecking rage, on this night of calm
The chaos plane vortexes him here
While lightning plays corporeal games
The dark one's preys on the innocent one

The thunder clashes, as she pants for breath
As the shadow chases the princess soul
Turning the corner, fear stabs her heart
His face sends her shrieking in pain
The blood curdling scream fills the stars
As they drip with her very blood
Flinching as her soul gets ripped from her heart
And phasing out as the mind crumples in pain
Laying there feeling naked to all
With a raped mind and molested heart ...
Looking out of his eyes she stares to the sky
To see the night has passed away
He passes her no phasing her sight
And she wonders ...
Who is this mind sorrowing fiend?
He, is Stalker

35. Shadows

The shadow… an ethereal man
Slips through cracks
The world is the childhood playground
Gripping a heart
Pure, lovely
Rippling through the air
Watching her,
And waiting
For a time when the darkness comes
She sleeps in peace
Not knowing what's there
The door is locked
Yet he enters
The window is closed
Yet he enters
With ghostly silence
A wisp of the wind
He enters her sanctum
She awakens …
The timber wolf howls to the forsaken moon

36. Sickness

This uncomfortable feeling
In my soul
Leaves me empty
Not quite whole
Like a giant burden
I carry with me
Every time your there
I feel like this great need to be
Sorrow plants seeds
In my heart
When I can't see you
When we part
Continuously torn away
I can barely cope
With my day
Array of sunshine
Touching my mind
An angel now, a demon to bind
What is this feeling?
Where is it coming from?
Feels so cursing
Feels now like my life is done
Why can't I get you out of my head?
My insanity is slipping from me
Filling with your thoughts instead
What is this sickness?
Where is the remedy?
I think I'm dying, can barely breath
All I want is for you to be with me
Dag nam it!

37. Kingdom

Where in the light do you hide?
Oh, angel of the beautiful night
Come into lights absence
And feel its powered grace
Listen to the stars dark omen songs
Hear them whisper you name
Enter the dark lord's gates
Which open before you
Walk into the velvet night court
Let them crown you
With a crown of fire
Receive the power to rule your kingdom
Where midnight creatures and shadows
Worship your name

38. Secrets

The final light of dusk
Is soaked up into the satin night
Ending another day of lies
Opening the window to the night of truth
Yet what truths lie in the shadows
That stalk you in this time of fear
They carry the world's deceptive lies
And the truths you always wished to hide
All the secrets that you keep
They know them

39. Beneath the Mask

I am life, I am death
I am the beginning, I am the end
Beginning of what? Who knows?
End of what? Who knows?
I am a reflection in everyone's mind
So, I am what they want me to be
Thus, I am Stalker a shadow in night
No one has seen my face beneath this mask
For they don't dare to look
Nor should they, but should they?
They will be frightened by which they find
For the loneliness and peace could cause them to cry
I am my own beauty
I am my own love
I am my own hatred
I am my own self
But who shall dare to see who I am?
Who knows?

40. Beauty and the Shadow

Sunlight
Those cursed golden rays
Warming my cold silver skin
I recoil into the shadows
With outstretched hand
Cursing Apollo with horrid black talons
My long black shagged hair
My shield against the warmth
Cast my blood bead eyes to the rock earth
To hide in shame
From all the pain
Yet … Behold!
The sunlight dies
What new fire claims the day?
An angel, God has sent an angel
In form of human flesh
An aura of fire gives her wings
The hair, blows like velvet in the breeze
An outstretched hand, so gentle
Eyes that hold entire worlds
Yet I must hide
Me, King of Shadows
From the Queen of Beauty
My wretched heart
She would never accept
Watch as she goes,
In peaceful silence

41. Stalker's Praise

All hail the shadows!
From where the master was born
Long live his name on our lips
May his thoughts ever echo in our hearts
Hail he who rose in the midst of tyranny
To oppose his princess mother
To take back his father land
And the name raped from him
Hail he who conquered the stars
And immortalized himself in their fire
Hail the shadows!
Hail the master within them!

Long live the Shadow King
All hail the Stalker

42.
Nighttime enshrouds me
It's dark love so tempting
Drawing me to voided life
No love, no emotion, no soul
Animated corpse I can feel
Hate calling to me
Mysterious voices from an ethereal gap
Pull me to the wolfen moon
I can't feel you anymore
Can't view your pretty face
Emit your pain to me
I couldn't really care
Light-life sucking black-hole heart
Feeds off turmoil
I can't feel you anymore
So much time spent hating
A reflective life
Of the demons in your soul
Don't see my own face at all
Just a pair of eyes staring back at me
Beating myself with your hand
Create reasons for me to repulse you
Molest my own nimble heart
To keep it from feeling
Make in bleed
Make it hurt
I don't want to feel it anymore
… feel you

43.
A joy divine slays the bravest hero
A sword so sharp that we don't know its strength
Its diplomacy forces us into the enemies' cannons
Driving us for wonderful peace, and ending up in bitter war

44. Torture

You stood there gazing in my eyes
You stood there laughing at me
My heart stabbed and bleeding
Life force pumping out of me
Tearful scorn no one would help
They all joined you, laughing
My heart is filled with you
Anger and vengeful rage
My body wanting to lash out
But I can't, due to your bondage
Controlling what I can of my mind
Try to despise and hate you
Uncontrolled dreams make me want you
Making me hate you all the more
I just want to mess you up
For everything you've done to me

45.

Dear child
Please forgive me
For all the pain I caused
See in your eyes the hurt
My hand has beaten in you
Violent voice of hatred
Lashing out in vengeance
Stabbing your heart
With this anger
Feel the pain with you
As angels constantly rape me
Even this dark lord be weak
Every day in my mind I die
For memories of those days
Dark storms harass my life
When my soul was invaded
A pretty face I trusted
Now always haunts me
Poison constantly pains me
Lion always mauls at me
So much pain in my life
It was nothing about you
That caused me to cause this torment
All I see is her face
Destroying me
Need to fight my demons
Who attack me through all of you
Can you forgive me?
For killing you?

46. Stalker Again

Small child weeping there
About some thought so lost
See those eyes
Terror filled and scared
Look in these eyes
See my face looking back at me
My world has died once again
While I break down upon this child
Feel the pain inside
Digging in my heart
This old hate has flared again
Where my soul died before
Feel myself falling away
Can't recover from these dreams
Old dreams that haunt
Raping the immortal soul
Dried blood has flamed away
Burned from the inside
Yet all I can see of this child
Is me

47. Control

Standing there innocently and sweet
A living illusion of tranquility
With a small, closed mind
Running a fantasy world
Believing that you are in control
But someone is pulling your strings
Someone is letting you believe you reign
Yet we are in control
Subconsciously, unknowing you obey us
The fear generated in your mind
Pushes you away from us
Always where we don't want you to be
Going where we want you to go
You don't come near so you do not see
When we come you don't speak in humble serenity
Can't you see we're in control?
Open up from your ignorant world
Fearing us is worshipping us
Continue to live in your puny world
Where we can continue to run your life

48.
The daytime is a lie
    Deceptive, and pleasing to the eye
The night-time is the truth
    Which we are afraid to explore

49. Were-Wolf

Bit last night by deceptive lies
I can feel something growing in me
It wishes to break out, roar out
It wishes to hunt in the merciless night
None would suspect to be such a beast
By looking at this human flesh
They continue to pound, rape and beat
Till the demon inside is released
Be careful that you didn't piss it off
Be sure you won't be devoured
Because it's coming after you
It's coming now to get you
There is no running from it
There is no hiding from it
For it knows your mind
With a second nature to hunt and stalk
You think your safe in your heaven
It's coming can you feel it hunting you?

50.
Never doubt your enemy
For it is that which will destroy you
Not your enemy
Suspect everything
Assume nothing
For assumption breed mistakes

51. Tell Me

My mind is thumping like a time-bomb
I don't even know what I did wrong
Tried asking everyone
No one seems to want to tell me

T'was treading home in innocence
No thoughts on my entrapped mind
'Till I saw a magical, angelic image
That threw me off my feet
Before I even came back to my senses
I was public enemy number one
My dignity was raped from me
Now I'm underground and unforgiven
For a sin that I didn't commit
What have I done?
Why do they keep me hanging here?
They all say I have been pardoned
So, where's my certificate?
But they still laugh at me
Whistle at me and harass me
I just wish they'd stop messin' with me
And tell me what I've done
So I can avenge myself
For what I haven't done

My mind in s thumping like a time-bomb
I don't even know what I did wrong
Tried asking everyone
No one seems to want to tell me

52. Faith

What shall I say?
When the souls don't listen
I cannot explain
To a door closed mind
What makes me believe
And why you should also
I believe in a future
I believe in a truth
I believe in a salvation
I believe in you
When I saw you standing there
I couldn't help but utter a prayer
Hoping my faith would not abandon me
Yet what shall I say?
When the world doesn't trust me
For the faith I do hold
That extends to the heavens above
I believe in a future
I believe in a truth
I believe in a salvation
I believe in you

53. I Came Back

Sent away into the void
A despised diseased animal
A contagious plague bore from you
Sunk your claws into my heart
Fed of the flesh of my bones
Burning alive, no hope, no light
But I have come back, for you
You cannot hide from me
Everywhere you go, I see you
Those pieces of me still with you
Everywhere you go, I feel you
My undead presence haunting you
You can't run, you can't hide
I'm coming for you
Fear is holiday you can't afford
Worthless life can't pay the price
Pitiful emotions don't matter much
Not even angels guard you
Nothing left to live for
As you cry and cry all night long
Solemnly realizing…
I have come back for you
You have shared your curse
It's come back on you
Messed with the wrong child of man
For now, I'm coming for you
I'll feed on your flesh
While I bathe in success
Molest your soul to the bitter end
'Till you never forget my face
Send you on a one-way trip to hell
I have come back for you

54. Where Am I Going Now?
Wait
I'm falling here now
Into this abyss, I think called love
It's so cold
It's so lonely
Where am I going now?
I see the shadows
At the top of my grave
Feeling the tears showering down on me
It's so cold
It's so lonely
Where am I going now?
Feel a presence at my side
Reaching out to me
Is it God?
Is it Jesus?
Is there someone out there who loves me?
It's so cold
Loves fire has frozen over
It's so lonely
I feel abandon here alone at my side
Where am I going now?
To heaven ...
This curse weighs me down from flying
Where am I going now?

55.

I wish my soul could reach out to you
On this night of storm and chaos
Take one moment of tranquility out of time
Share with you the song my heart wants to sing
But I can't touch your soul
Because you're so far away from me
You dance there
I stand by watching so quietly
My soul gets disturbed standing there
It wants to be there with you
But I can't touch your soul
Because you're so far from me

56.

Some may ask what I've seen
Wanting to know my horrid dreams
Barely can force an answer
Screaming as I speak out of fear
Cringing in a lighted room
From flickering and dancing shadows
Tell them to run, run far from here
An evil lurks you can't imagine
All it wants is to feed off you
Feed off your soul, feed off your mind
Why it's spared me I don't know
Furious storm as its joyride goes
Judging all the innocent
Letting the guilty free
I've been courted and judged now
To live through this cursed hell
Pray that it executes you
A picnic park, where you'll be happy to be

I've seen the face of the devil
Beautiful yet deceptive it's true
Walking around us in the day
Mingle with it, making it proud
Small facts come from one truth
That I've seen the face of you
I've see the face of the devil
Because I've seen the face of you

57. Tomorrow

The knife of injustice
Lodged into my heart
All its intense, searing pain
Bleeding through all my veins
Carved as a ruby heart
I know when tomorrow comes
I'll be dead once again
No one there to ease the pain
No one there to help my soul
Rest at peace
How I lived that evil night
I cannot recall
As demons danced on my head
And on my heart
They bathed in my blood
And ate at my flesh
As the powers of hatred
Consumed my damned soul
When I woke
Found myself staring at my own grave
And now that I'm back
You want to puppet me again
I don't think so
You want me to be there with you
To be there like a faithful dog
That will heed to your every command
I will not fall in love with you again
I will not lend my heart to you again
Go molest yourself once again
You stupid demon
Where were you
When I was crying here
Where were you
When I was screaming here
Where were you
When I was thinking

How am I going to live through today?
To see tomorrow
Where were you?

58.

Beautiful angel of shimmering grace
Standing there in her glorious light
Blessing hearts with a simple "hello"
All pretense of evil leaves the soul
A blessed smile that never dulls
Every time bringing joy again
Never judging wretched men
Always giving second chances to prove their worth
Song voice carried by the gentle wind
Speaking with pure eloquence
A gift to the earth no one deserves
Her aura of beauty blankets her
Lost souls find their way
By the guiding light that shines
In a world of chaos
There exists an island of tranquility
That everyone finds
By the brightest star that shines
The heavenly host whispers the name
That gives searchers hope
Remembering that portrait of majesty
Beautiful angel of shimmering grace

59. Bondage

Wretched tears of poisoned blood
Painting pictures in ominous circles
Of tortured pasts in a creviced earth
Dreams are raped to conformed dreams

Death's silent grace offers such hope
To escape this mortal bondage of freedom
Finally passing beyond this life
And smile in humble victory

Burdens cuffs wrapped in red tape
Sign of bondage in lights shadow
Can't fly with these trimmed wings
Awaiting judgment to rain on me

60.
Where did the angels go?
No light for them to bask in
Consumed every source of hope
Fighting off our righteous guardians
Dying to own self pride
God's dead in our hearts
How pathetic our souls are
To be that wretched
To be that vile
Where did the angels go?

61.
Standing at the edge of no where
Without a destination in sight
Groveling at some useless hope
Where nothing ever comes true
Blasting a mind in a pointless quest
Of uncertain truth that may not exist
Beholding a whitewashed realm
That sucked in some twisted dreamland
Needing to reach out to a star
But weighed down by God knows what
Frenzied fists of unequaled rage
Pounding the angry soul
Slumps to the merciless ground
And cries, despised, unloved

62.

Weight of life so much
The journey from here is so hard
I tried to look in the eyes of grace
Nothing's there
Sword of Darkness runs through me
Steals away this life of mine
Steals away this pain of mine
I woke this morning
To discover I was still alive
Cried out to my God for mercy
It hurts so much
To live under the face
Of that unloving grace
Loneliness overtakes me
Hauls me off to a foreign land
Where emotion beats me
And rapes me at its leisure
Hurts so much to keep loving
To keep praying for peace
No one wants to come and save me
From my captor of grace
Why can't I leave this gothic life?
Full of darkness, of death
Can't even see past my own turmoil
To see that face every day ...
It hurts

63.
You face haunts me through everyday
Yet what I want is to be near you
It hurts to be in your presence
All I want, is to hear your voice

64. Reject

Why do I try?
All I see is your back side
Constantly turning sun ward
Leaving me in your shadow
Lonely heart rips at me
Slashes me like paper
Can feel myself bleeding
Love has hurt me again
What do you want from me?
There's nothing to surrender
In this blackened void of life
All I have is my soul
But you don't want that
Don't want it, it's not good enough
At least you kindly told me
To leave you alone
Instead of throwing me off this ledge
Into the ravine of hate
Here I am again
Bleeding out my dignity
For some reason unknown to me
You're still there
What have I done?
To deserve this hated rejection
From your Venusian race
Not a Martian no
Too good for that
I'm a distant Plutonic mess
Cold and dark, unwanted
Never feel the warmth of anything again
Left frozen in emotional hell
For some reason I still care
Love has hurt me again
Why do I try?
To talk to you every time you're near
Want to see you smile

See you happy
Joyous chorus fills my heart
When you are near me
Catch you looking at me
See something there, some star
But what do you want?
Don't want my soul
Everything that I am
All I have is me
Run down piece of junk
No bounty to my name
Don't know me as good as you think
You judge me so quickly
What do you want?
What do you want me to do?
What do you want me to say?
Can feel myself bleeding
Bleeding out my dignity
See something there, some star
Love has hurt me again
Come to me
    No go away
Let me near you
    Don't want me anyways
Let my embrace you
    Stupid fantasies of love
Let me inside your heart
    You haunt my dreams
Let me ...
    Love has hurt me again

65.
Night is now fallen
My heart so wants to sing
Of evil days and evil minds
Attacking my soul raping me blind
All these things that I see
Masked lies thrown at me
Feel something out there
Somewhere
What more is going on?
In all of their minds?
Their deceptive truths unconvincing
So obvious what's happening
Why keep lying to me
You hate me, I can see it
In your eyes when you look at me
I can feel it
When you mock me
I know you mean it
They all laugh at my misfortunes
No one cares at all
They may hate me
Their lies don't brainwash enough
Feel something out there
Somewhere
Why do they all treat me this way?
Dirty dog to beat and kill
Like I know nothing
As though I'm a retarded fool
Why are you treating me this way?
You hate me, I can see it
In your eyes when you look at me
I can feel it

66. Fuel, Blood and Water

Are you ready?
To take me by the hand
Are you ready?
To play emotions instead
Do you want so bad
To mess around some more?
Tool me off
Wrench my brain until I bleed
Screw my conscious till I scream
Rack me up until I die
If I didn't flow down streams of life
Admiring the beauty I see
Forgiveness of sorts may fall short
Of the buoy that'd I throw
The sun can't shine without fuel
No light would emit itself to you
Heart is useless without blood
No river left to paddle on
Run fire through my veins
See me wriggle there in grief
When will I get the fuel, blood and water?
From you to live
What more must I endure of this?
Agonizing millennia long period
Fooled emotions despairing
Need to fill, need to feel
All the simple essentials
That I need

67. Tower

Stand there precious
Tower standing in the air
Stone cold touch chaffs me away
Never thought it'd feel like this
No conqueror can touch you
Won't let anyone in
Am I poison?
Am I disease?
What are you saving yourself from?
Don't wanna give up
Rusted door holds me back
No key to enter in
No answer to the gargoyles gong
That just stares at me
Can't resist the aura of life
That surrounds and grows upon
Shimmering light from deep inside
Beautiful fire of love

68.
Feel so pushed away
Exiled within my own mind
Feel so strange
This war drum inside me
Just gotta let it out
Scream out my pain
So few words are killing me
Discover a unique soul
Desperately trying to find
Yet all it does is beat me
Puts an ice pick through my heart
Won't let me hear
Such a beautiful voice
This little punk freak
Not worthy I know
Just hurts so bad
Feel a surge pulsing in me
Forces out these tears
That are drowning me
Why do I try so hard?
All it does it hurt me

69. Uneasy Peace

Unsure of these humble days
It's all too quiet
Makes me so uneasy
Used to the noise of war
Made me soft again
Temptation reels me in
See a star in the distant sky
Shed a tear of sadness for the pain
Entrapped in a cocoon
Can't escape from this
Feel so dead
Need some life again
Unable to fire bloody cannons
In search of this
Boredom so terrible
It aches my heart
As I quietly waste away
Dreaming of feats of heroes
The sword of which used to slay
Lays no more than a reach away
Yet I hesitate
I know that path has grown over
I am not too tired it, not yet
No matter how I tire
Of this uneventful existence
Even as I lost my soul in the fight
Something liked it better
I must stay in this peace
Clouds cover my thoughts
As storms of sorrow fall about me
Heart wants to explode
It'd be more exciting than sitting here
In this corner listening to the rain

70. Love Song of the Unforgiven

The days subtle dawning
Arouses my damned soul
But this day means now nothing
Yet it had once before
When I was innocent and pure
With a dream non-perishing
It gave me hope and fire
That dream was you
But now I'm unforgiven
Due to your twisted soul
My heart got thrown from heaven
As I died along the roadside
I now no longer know what love is
Only that I felt it once ago
When my hands were unscarred
From a blood promise I made
To always care and be for
That now is poison to me
Your thought never left my eyes
Everywhere I went, there you were
Even death couldn't have stopped me
That's why I perished and returned
But you never noticed my decease
And kept laughing at your lie of me
You continued to laugh at my pain
While I died in shame
All the time I thought I was crazy
To continue to love you
So now I question
If holding to your dream is worthy
Because if I died again tonight
I owe it to you that no one would care
I have no reason to love you
You stole that away from me
I cried out all my tears
Easing pain unthinkable

But it never helped at all
For now, I'm unforgiven
Now here I'm lying
Drowning in such agony
You still don't leave my thought
What is this I'm feeling?
Even though you can never share this
Because now I'm unforgiven

71.
The howling moon asks for flesh
You hear its whisper in your soul
See the immortal sins of the herds
That feed in the field of love
Their foolish games, watch them
Pathetically, trying to amuse
Gods of pansy playfulness

'The blood of ages flows so sweet
Come, drink from us.'
Are we actually ignorant enough
To sing such blasphemy?
Yet Vampires and Ghouls
Whose hearts drip in blood
Try to incinerate our thought

The howling wolf, summons us!
A white alpha, with a new beginning
Do we dare not heed its call?
Shadows embrace us to play stalkers games
And be called to a land
Where no immorality falls
The land of glorious death

So now, brethren of night
Whom they have prejudiced
Let us heed this call
A holy task, that we
Dare not refuse
Go! Purify the Earth!
Liberate it from these tyrants

72.
Alone at night with weeping tears
You feel as though there's no one who loves you
All your hopes and cares of all the years
With nobodies' shoulder to cry on
Look into the shadows lurking there
You'll see you are not alone
Beaded eyes of thirsty blood

73. Part of Me

Mirror reflection on my soul
Creating illusions in the mind
Savage beast influencing me
I cannot love, I only hate
Thunder head rolling into me
Lashing out in exquisite pain
Anger fuels the machine of rage
Corruption, out of me, has been made
This is the quiet part of me
You are a part of me
Demon slayer has been slain
Ray of hope has fled away
I thought that I could find peace
In this unforsaken place
Blinding sunlight trying to save me
Hiding from this blasphemous salvation
No savior here in this damned world
Nothing in this realm, nothing in this life
This is the quiet part of me
You are a part of me
Abandon, broken highway
Walking this long way alone
Unforgiven saints beating me down
No guiding hand to take me home
Lonely heart beating foreign blood
Something invading me that I do not know
It despises me, its eating me
No one is here yet someone is killing me
This is the quiet part of me
You are part of me
Unclear destiny drives my soul on
A familiar, yet unknown face
This is a part of me

74. Why

Why did you come into my life
A runaway freight train
Cleansed my soul from darkness
A purifying fire
Why does my mind prey on you?
Why do I want to see your face?
When did I succumb to this?
Accepted me in my damnation state
Went out of your way to make me smile
All I want is you, all I feel is you
You are all that I need
I still cannot comprehend
What you did for me
You freed me from bondage
Made me whole

75.
Take a piece of reality away, and all you're left with is a dream

76. Youth
The world lives
The world breathes
But it doesn't matter
All we see is ourselves
Our own appearances
Is all that consume us
Do what to do to be accepted
Lying to and about ourselves
We drape masks of glory up on our faces
Till it becomes a part of us
And we brainwash ourselves
Then suddenly we awake
To a blinding light
Lucifer's burning torch
We believe that we carry burdens
To us they are heavy
But we are yet young
We do not possess the strength
To proceed with this stress
So many little things poke into us
In return we revert the brain to mush
The only world which exists is our own
Nothing else matters
Only ourselves
Catch 22's horde around us
"Save the trees! Save the oceans!"
Yet we want, so we take
So, we destroy
"Equality!"
Yet we degrade ourselves
The world lives
The world breathes
Yet all we see is ourselves

77.

Rest here, lay down my child
Your world falls down around you
Shed your tears
Water the hate crop in your soul
Try to rip the burdens off of you
But don't hand them to me
Your world is so demon plagued
Convinced yourself of your own grief
Why have you chosen to be blind?
Open up your closed eyes
Go see your beauty
And the light you shine to the world
You conceive this small world
Is the only one in your mind
Everything that happens is on you
Open your closed eyes
You are not that only one here

78.

Rain roars down around me
The silver moon ever haunting
Evil howls sing out the stars
Tears pitter-patter on the ground
Angels have fled to heaven
No guardians protecting me
Approaching shadows terrorizing
No soul dares reach out to me
Alone here crying
I'm dying in my own blood
Ice pick of hate in my heart
Has poisoned my red veins
I feel it, crawling up my spine
Tentacles suffocating
Vampire leach feeding
Banshee's scream, laughing
Mocking me, degenerating me
Crying out to God
Why won't he answer?

79.
Prancing through the lights glorious day
Believing now we all follow the way
All the bastards we can see
Are deceiving suckers just as you and me
Pitiful emotions that we feel
Swearing secrets to each other with a golden seal
Minds so single tracked, so closed
Little voices to our souls, roads propose

80.
Thus, we have stopped believing in shadows
And seen the light
Therefore, we are born
Therefore, we must fight

81.
Realize that your entire life
You have been lied to
Each night when you close your eyes and dream
Your mind is raped
And so, I call on you
To stand and take back your dignity
And we shall shed black tears
On this glorious day
For we know what has begot this joy

82.

Pondering I wait here
While unveiling the faces of those around me
All the truths they keep to themselves
How much of it do they believe?
What portions of that belief
Is some god's manipulative work?
Is it money?
Is it television?
Social pressure?
I think of myself and wonder
What clouds have I wrapped myself in?
Anger facilitates my soul, no wonder
For foolish choices I have made
Do these faces also suffer
From this erotic disease?
Do they realize who they are?
Or what they are?
The world manipulates all of us
To morph us into something else
A master teaching his dog new tricks
And rewarding his afterwards
We have all been lured, I think
Subconsciously we realize it
That's why we are angered
We blindly see we are not in control
How sad

83.
Crying out
I'm standing here
In the mornings darkness
I can feel the world
Reaching out to touch my soul
The evil presence
That it emanates
I can feel the darkness
Dominating your mind
Demons pawn you
In some earthly game
You agent of evil
You agent of pain
A whore in a world
Where you believe you're a king
Awaken dark beauty
Wake up from your sleep
Lift up the veils
That weigh on your eyes

84.
I did not come here to fall in love with you
For I was called here from afar
When I got here you were in that place
My heart could not help but call to you

My heart was led here to this place
To a place I did not know
I followed blindly here by faith
Scared and wondering how I came
You were standing in this world
Calmly standing there
Emanating presence enshrouded you
Welcoming, comforting
I pushed away, not wanting
For I did not want to give to thee

85.
Guiding light
Illuminating my broken path
Leads me on, forward, forward
Blindly I follow
This goal of hope
And its golden rays
Pull me forth
Interpretations are so wrong
My ignorant assumptions
Have caused my fall
Assumption
Breeds the ultimate descensions
And here I am
Once again following
This unknown coming
The future is all that is left
The only rung I hang on to
Having become a slave to it
To the angel held within
I follow the future
Being subservient to it
But it does not matter to me
For to me
It promises hope

86. Call Out

Feel the energy flow through you
Let the psycho out in you now
All the voices cannot be
Demanding you to call out
See the world collapse around you
You're not crazy the world is
Burn things like the leprechaun told you
Messing up the other psychos
Call out, what your heart tells you
Piss off, everyone else
Destroy, something you really hate
Call out ... call out
Living out our quiet lives
Mindless drones without names
Wandering soullessly through this plane
Called sane, while we're really insane
Living shells, impenetrable hell
No one is allowed inside
Not even love can break this life
Only hatred of this life
Call out, what your heart tells you
Piss off, everyone else
Destroy, something you really hate
Call out ... call out
Call out

87. Freak

You don't dare to look at me
Not best child's brain food
You imagine me falling to hell
As I am just one more disease
Watch me pollute your mind
And steal your sanity from you
Now open your eyes and see your world
Is the world of the freaks
You continue to push me aside
Not looking in my eyes
What do you see when you look at me?
Just a normal kid in jeans, in shirt
But look at my soul
In the dark demon crypt
That I'm a freak of freaks
Even different to differents
I am not your average bum
Fear me in revenant plea
Open your single track eyes
And watch the freak show
Try not to shake in terror
For I'm only a freak

88. Puppy
There are reasons why we run away

We will run from you
Master's and mistresses too
You keep me on a damn leash
Rejecting me all day
Feeling alone and unloved
I had feared you
I had loved you
Now I hate you
You treat me like a puppy dog
Not ever letting go
I didn't bring your paper
So, you beat me to the ground
Throwing rocks at me to shut up
When I never made a peep in the night
Smacking me when I defend myself
From the beatings you rape me with
I continue to dream of the day
When I will run free
The time that I can howl again
Without human retribution
But it's just a vision
Since you won't leave me be

There are reasons why we run away

89. War

What have I said to you?
What have I ever done to you?
What kind of curse am I now?
Where is this peace the world keeps promising me?
Love is a power divine
Yet what has it done for my life?
Nothing but pain, has it hurled on me
Nothing but its hate, exposed to me
War is the constant in our lives
What the hell are we fighting for?
You hate me, and I hate you
Your pretty face I'll hold as I watch it burn
Hate the power that has consumed my heart
Everything I see is stained in blood
Brainwashed people tools of devilish love
Your face now looks like everyone else's
Quaking in fear now, I see I am dying
I see now my soul is morphing like yours
Yet I will not die hear quiet, alone
War is the constant in our lives
I now know what I am fighting for
You hate who I am, I hate who you are
Your pretty souls I'll conform to mine
It's war
We Are Resisting

90. Alive?

I had stumbled through this day
But all I see is a great haze
I can remember a whole lot of nothing
I think I may know my name
Phasing as I walk
No one seems to see me
I cry out aloud
No one seems to hear me
A piece of reality
Has been taken away
Dancing through what's left
All that's left is this dream
I know I am alive
I feel my cold skin
Yet I'm treated like I'm dead
Not noticed at all
I noticed why suddenly
I saw myself there
Life no longer flowed through my veins
Eyes were empty and hollow
Everyone walked around me
No help, no caring people
A ray of truth struck me
I remember why
I forgot I was alive
Refusing to live my life
My mind convinced I'm dead
So now the shell is lying there
Can't help but cry here alone
Yet no one can hear me
No one cares
No one knows

91. Bride of Cain

Drinking foul enemy blood
Awakening a quiet beast
Consuming the holy soul
Flinging her into righteous bloodlust
The lord of murder smiles down
Upon the loyal heart
Gifting her with godly blessings
A heroine to her nation
Advancing their cause
She not need a cause
To go to shed blood
Just the order of her god
To bathe in orgasmic plea
In conquered enemies blood
To please her murderous lord
Thrusts herself into conflict
Among flashing swords and spears
Soft flesh does not resist the poison
She digs into the hearts
Smiling in glee as her enemies wriggle
In frenzied pleasure molests her body
Standing after the deed is done
Sacrifices the survivors to Cain
Her lord, father and husband
Then takes the blood in her flask
To drink once more for her god

92. Child of Blood

Unsure eyes piercing the slitted darkness
Awaiting the roar of malicious beasts
Sharp tongued friend awaits at his side
To water the fields with opponents' blood
Ancient, burdened beast of old
Waits as such to drink red wine
To keen its senses
Arousing its innermost desires
Awaiting behind the banner of blood
Where wailing banshees scream
Needing to feast in an orgy of gore
To appease the bloody handed god
Yet he silently waits calm and humble
Elegant defender mounted solemnly on his arm
Hefty ore of precious stones
Gifted to him from trials of war
Perking up he hears them come
As do his entire hoard
Drawing two vipers from the quiver of snakes
He charges forth releasing his dual serpents

93. Rainfall

Descending grace raining on me
Cooling my hate heated soul
Offering peace to bustling minds
Casting a symphony of pure mourning
Silent pitter-patter echoing around
Softening the war-time minds
Feeding the earth, giving it life
So it will be green with life tomorrow
Gentle breeze blanketing all
Calming the frenzied beast
Swirling color into the sky
When the warmth of light comes
Reminding us of old promises
Of life, of its precious cycles

94. Cry of the Earth

Holy rain fall on earth
Cleanse this impure world
Wash away this cursed plague
Consuming, engulfing this ball
The murderous pestilence
Destroying all it sees
To live in fantasy lands
Where nothing really truly exists
Believe they are masters
Of the universe whole
So they judge and condemn others
Yet saying they are one
Their brittle peace between themselves
Is only a mere illusion
They believe in unholy religions
Where they think they are gods
They claim to live life and be unique
Yet rules are set down
For what is allowed for different
And what is different is monstrous
What brainwashed children
Who slew their parents
In humble rebellion
To prove their worthless might
Now there is no-one left to blame
With only brothers and sisters remaining
They shed sibling blood
And believe they administered justice
Holy rain fall on earth
Cleanse this world with fire
Purify it of all cursed ones
Wash them away

95. Here I Wait

Sorrowed I wait here
I can feel your soul by me
My heart grows heavy
Patience fire, blazes bright
By this light shine
May a spirit be drawn to me
Alone I'm falling
To my own blasting hell
Will an angel come to save me?
Come rescue me
Dreams are racing
Through peaceful fantasies
Where I live with fire
Warming, comforting
Come to me, my angel
Fill my heart, with your love
Ever since I first saw you
You shone with holy fire
My heart cried out to you
But you did not answer me
So now, I keep calling
And I wait, alone

96. Heretics

Heresy
It is time for it to come
The judgment from above
Let apocalyptic fires rain
Down on us all
Let it all burn
Purify the earth
All the sin of the world
Let the rats burn
Cleanse yourself O earth
Immunize this plague
Don't let it consume you
Rain fire on us all

97. Ascension

I can't see, but I can feel
A holy power
Consuming my soul
It's calling me
Far away
Someplace, somewhere
Little voice
Inside my heart
To go, go
Into this hell freakish world
World claws
Clasping my flesh
Holding me, to the ground
To the place
Where I must go to be
Raised up above this worldly hell
To be judged, so I can judge the earth
Let go of me
Earthly tempters
Leave me be
Dark voices
So I can ascend
To the heavens

98. The Prisoner
Dragged off
In bounds, in chains
All my freedom lost
To a soul in a far off realm
A realm of purity and light
There she is standing there
Behind a wall of glass
Untouchable, unreachable
Demons carrying me off
To a destiny I know I want
Yet for some reason
When the angels halo
Comes to my mind
I don't wish to die
But to live
Her soul comes to caress my mind
It feels soft and comforting
When it leaves
I feel raped and violated
She just stands there
Coldly staring in my heart
Staring, staring
With the flick of her wrist
It all goes black

99.
Living out these blasted times
These hurting times
Trying to cope and not to hate
Just wanting to find my own way
Through this life, through the day
Emotion pool is drowning me
Don't want to feel, don't want to care
A holy lamb comes from above
Has my heart, and I want it again

I don't wanna live, I don't wanna die
I feel this pain, please tell me why
I don't wanna live, I don't wanna die
Why all this grief? Send me relief

100. Power Lie

What can make a warrior cry?
Cause the demoness to flee
To break unbearable bondage?
And cause a man to break out?
Is there a force so strong?
That all these things come true?
Broken hearts find mending
With gentle hand of healing
Cursed minds are purified
Blackened souls are whitened again
Evil men bend to mush
Princes give up entire realms
In name of some great power
They are willing to die for
Can someone say what this is?
That the greatest of all power
And renown spirits crumble?
For this heart core shame?
I don't believe in this thing called love
Just doesn't make sense to me
How could someone care that much?
To abandon their dignity?
To worship a name that's insignificant
Give up everything they could have been
Just think of this stupid concept
Where men make fools of themselves
And for what and for who?
So that an ominous dagger of death
Can be plunged in your heart
And you'll die alone in the night
You won't care 'cause you believe in this crap
Not one thing has love done for me
Except let me watch myself bleed

101. The Fence

Iron cage running onward, onward
Holding the precious future in
Creating an illusion of protection
While blocking out realities truths
Twisted wire of poisoned pain
Deters us from finding ourselves
Out there in the great beyond
This iron wall doesn't let us touch
Ball of fire that hangs on the blue wall
Reaches through this grey divider
Enlightening some few blessed minds
That dare to climb up high
Daring to escape new found hell
To run free, away from there
The truth they find is not heaven
Yet not the hell from where they came
The outside looked bright and cheery
As the world they had just left
But it's an arid field cracked and dead
No sunlight shines on the ground
A blood red star emits its eerie light
Over this freakish fact
Though in the middle of this dead plain
Lies a single spark of hope
That has forced its way to earth
Protruding an aura like nothing before
The fantasy that had just been left
Holds nothing like this
The truth now is seen
This white rose in the middle of hell
Unlike all the red roses they've only seen
They approach the iron wall
Tempted to go back
To be a slave in heaven
Or rule in hell
Are the decisions they face

While they are now free
To reclimb the iron cage
This time to face poisoned death
Or perhaps to preach salvation
To all the ones who did not come
Still living in la la hell
Some go over, some stay back
Some die, some live
Now facing eternal retribution
At the hands of fellow man
Still trapped in dream land
Ignorant of the truth
But they fight to break the iron cage
To stop watching shadows on the wall
Let the truth be known
Free the human race from self-oppression

102. Get A Life

What do you want from me?
Bashing my head in oozing out the red goo
Taking a power trip on my sorry butt
Using you demon hand to jack the funky monkey man
Sucking out my life force
Forcing me to spew
Raging out your problems
On me now
Get a life
Go beat someone else
I hate you, and your attitude
I can't stand to be near you
Keep screwing with me
And I'll screw up all your thoughts
You may have the looks
You many have the friends
Doesn't change the solemn fact
That you're a dirt whore
If you don't stop
I'll beat your head in
That's being gracious
More than you deserve
Can't stand your ungodliness
You think you rule me
You don't
So, get a life
I hate you and who you are
You treat me like garbage
I'll make sure the tables change
Fire will rain down on you
Think you can escape my fury
Just try it
Summon down a hurricane to stalk you

103. Destiny

Waltzing down this road
Not too sure where it leads
All I know is to keep going
To just humbly see
Some things I do fear
Other things I don't
But this ache in my heart
Is terror I'm sure to be
I gaze to the blue grey horizon
Seeing premonitions of my past
Scream out my last step
I dare not go on
I'm tired of this all of this
I just want it to end
The next flashing moment
Gave me courage to keep going
I made a mess of my obligations
Thrown across the ground
I was kneeling before an angel
She softly spoke to me
Asked me if she could be mine
So now I walk ...
To find the future
I know where this road leads
'Tis my destiny

104. The Avengement

Reigning judgment on the people
Trying to fight back, yet they can't
Hordes of people heed the calling
Losing out on free salvation
Dig claws into your flesh wall
Stroke of hatred maims your soul
You can't run, you can't hide
Molest your body and watch you scream
Cast a demon in your mind
Watch you wriggle in explicit horror
Screaming for the burden of mercy
Pardon you, hear you freak in terror
Let the lightning sing to you
To the thunders malevolent song
Knowing what it is to be dead yet alive
Crying for your soul to die
Toss you into burning sulfur
Confessing now ...
I am avenged!

105. Let Me Fly

Swore I wouldn't fall into this pit
Convinced I flew away from this place
But currents of fate brought me back
Now I'm descending into this gaping pit
With no hope of escape
My wings are just imagined faith
That I can run away
From this hell born place
I feel so weighed down
Ball and chain is drowning me
I pray I'll be given the faith
To soar away, grace the stars with my wings
I wish I knew where I was going
These rock walls tell me nothing
I know that this is not right
There's something more, I know
I am a chosen strand of blood
With a Gentile cursed soul
I have been graced from on high
I feel unprecedented power pumping through me
So why am I falling now
I cry out to the heavens
Lift me up let me fly
Let me use this you've given me
I know you are out there
Lift me up let me fly

106. Confession

Woe to the soul that cries out yet not heard
A tearful heart watering fields of sorrow
The wolf is no longer hunting the prey
Blood has lost its favored taste
Tears have diluted the tainted blood
Also, the hate encoded within
The soul still cries out
Regretting the past, sorry for the past
Hoping the regretted will miraculously change
No hope is given, no faith can help

107. Imperial March

Hear them come
All in step, step by step
Right feet land
At the beat of the drum
The armies of shadows march
To the Imperial March
This season of blood
No man remembers
When almighty Caeser
Fell to the Grim Reapers blow
On that dark day of spring
The Ides of March
Spelt such doom
And the armies of shadows marched
To the Imperial March
Two millennia more past
When the shadows moved again
A child was born
Screaming into the world
The curse of Caeser
Ever upon him
So, armies of shadows marched
To the Imperial March
The child taken
And presented to God
Defiled the shadows
For the master not born to them
So, they punished him
With pain and despair
But yet they marched
To the Imperial March
Their Imperial master
Did return to them
To command his servants
So, the shadows marched
To the Imperial March

But the master fled
From his power throne
For innocent blood
To claim his own
Torn and beaten
Down was he
So, returning to his shadows
He plotted with glee
And the shadows marched
To the Imperial March
Again he left
Unknown why
Yet they remembered
The Ides of March
And their emperor's birth
The Imperial March
So, they continue to march
The Imperial March

108. Living Nightmare

You are the one
I am your shadow
I am your darkest nightmare
You are the angel
This demon feeds on
I'm unforgiven
My soul thrown from heaven

You rocked my world
With that damn smile
Then you raped my soul
Till I was nearly dead
Now I've come again
Into your night
As a living shadow
And a demon king

I'm the last
Of the living nightmares
So damn unfair
That it had to be you
But it's your problem
Not mine anymore
Because now I'm your problem
Now I'm you living nightmare

109. Dream Angel

I've always been weak to your smile
My heart could never give in to denial
Of the fact your thoughts are with me
And all this time I could never see
But it's done now I've lost
The war for love is too high the cost
I'll attempt to walk from your thought
Try to find the dignity I have sought
But I remember that sweet song
That made me love you for so long
I just walk back to where I left
I let the boat of peace to drift
My final salvation from love
Flies away like a white holy dove
Because I'm willing to pay the price
To see that face again lovely and nice
To feel your love never given
To watch you come down from heaven
For your my dream angel, I've seen in the night
Being in the presence of you feels so right
I can feel your heart beat
And every step taken by your feet
I can feel you soul at my side
I can't help but to feel such pride
For you're my dream angel girl
And I will always love you

110. No Matter

No matter how it hurts
No matter how you feel
No matter how you try
No way will you be forgiven
No matter how you moan
No matter how you scream
No matter how many tears you cry
No way will you be forgiven
No matter how you plead
No matter how you love
No matter how you bleed
No way will I forgive you
You caused me to fall from heaven
You cursed me with demonhood
You made me live in shadows
No way will you be forgiven

111. Dance With Me

Dance with me my angel
Smoothly playing your feet
On the dance floor mist
Fueled by some energy
That only comes from above
Smiling sweetly, carelessly
With no worry in life
Show me this peace
Let my hold you in my arms

Dance with me my angel
Make true my fantasies
Dance with me my angel
Dance with me

Wipe those tears away
Don't cry, just smile
Let me know in my heart
This is no fantasy

Dance with me
Dance with me
Dance with me my angel

112. Oppress

Shadowed the sun, no face to shine
Fought the storm, and blew me down
Tried to burn the soul of the earth
Washed me away with its tide
Was fighting the system
Bearing the sword of light
But the world doesn't want a savior
They want to die at an oppressor's hand
So, I ascend now to the dark throne
Reserved for my enlightened soul
To oppress the poor mortals
Watch them die by my hand
Hear their hearts scream
For non-existent mercy
And let these mice squeal
In ceaseless pain
After I've conquered my people with fear
The world machine will I destroy
Send out my angels
To destroy its demons
Corruption will be their salvation
Damnation to save their souls
I'll oppress the poor mortals
Watch them die by my hand
Hear their hearts scream
For non-existent mercy
Let these mice squeal
In ceaseless pain

113. Cry

I gazed into your world eye windows
To see them drowning in your pain
You wandered around the hallways
Looking rejected with such shame
My heart just suddenly cried out
Because it hurt to see you there
In such pain and anguish
My lonely heart could feel you there
Now when time comes to pass
And I'm the one there crying
I just pray that you will be there
With a shoulder for me to cry on
When I finally breathe my last breath
May your face be all I see
As I lie in your tender arms
Crying myself to final sleep
And when I'm lying in your arms
Will you cry when I'm gone?

I'll let you cry on my shoulder
Because you're a savior to my heart
I'll let you cry on my shoulder
Just let me die in your arms

114. I am Free

I was walking down life's road of pain
While death followed me everywhere
Like a slave living through this age
Hatred consumed my heart
But it wasn't until I saw you
Walking out of the sun rising horizon
With wings of fire
And a seal of truth
I can now say that ...
I am free
I am free from death
I am free from pain
I am free from sorrow
I am free
And when all this has passed away
When I dance in the stars with you
So my soul can be free all night
Which you helped me do
I now know that ...
I am free
I am free from life
I am free from night
I am free from this world
I am free

115.
What must I do?

What mountain must I cross?
To sit next to you again?
What ocean must I swim?
To see in your eyes of life once more?
What must I say?
To hear your song voice again?
Sat there next to you
In my day of sorrow
The way the wind whispered your name
I knew you must be angelic
The way you looked at me
I saw you were unique and special
Your voice and gentle laughter
Made my sorrow a day of joy
What mountain must I cross?
To sit next to you again?
What ocean must I swim?
To see your eyes of life once more?
What must I say?
To hear your song voice once more?

116. Alone

Looking out I phase the world
And escape to a land so far away
Where all accept me for who I am
And my dark veil is a playful lie
Alas that is only an inspired thought
The real world is a tone deaf song
Searching, pawing into the void
Are there any people who care?
Right in my chest an empty heart
And this lonely child can't bear it
I see other couples, conquering the stars
Lingering here I cannot see
Of all the things I hide my face
Very ashamed because I am not sought
Every day I rise alone
Yet no one comes to heal this wound
Over time I've built a wall
Unknowing I believe it can bear the storm
But when lightning comes the wall will fall
And I stand here once more alone

117. I Stand

Here I stand all alone
The world is so monochrome
Black and white, night and day
Fate just works that way
Pin pricks with a trickled flood
The gray shades now stained in blood
Mortal child cries aloud
Virginity lost to the crowd
The demon child dies in pain
The love of man withers in vain
All the truth they know to be
Is what the gods let them see
Ignorant minds, passionate lies
Worshipping the dragon as it flies
Not knowing what lies beyond
The truth of love of which their not fond
This, that, right and wrong
All head to this war song
But given the choice of light or dark
They'd rather bear, the devils mark

118. Angel of Mine

I opened my eyes to see a world tainted in blood
Yet that wasn't all
I saw people's demons
Feeding off this vampires wine
My stomach churned my guts to cheese
I saw no sign of hope
So, I made my peace with God
As I saw the demon's hunger for my flesh
Crouched on one knee ready to die
I shook in fear at what came
A tear fell in desperate plea
Just to fall ... to an enlightened hand
Looking to this source of light in the dark
Another tear fell but of joy
The face of beauty itself gave hope
In this angel of mine
Now your name is on my mind all day
No dark creature can touch me
And no poison blood can kill me
For your name is holy, being from on high
Angel of mine ease my pain
Let me cry alone no more
May my burdens be lifted
Will you please heal my cracked open heart?
Angel of mine listen to my plea
In this world of lies
Where love is a dream
May this dream be all that I need in you
Angel of Mine

119. Mother Earth

Oh, great crystal ball of emerald and life
In a beautiful body with a soul of fire
Shining brighter than the stars combine
This twinkle of hope reaches the angels eye

This body with a soul all its own
Bringing life to the corners of hell
Its loveliness God had meant to be
To reach to other system souls as such

When all time has passed away
Its twinkle, stars still cannot beat
Death even fears this holy shine
What beauty where you created from?

Mother Earthen Terra, window to life
Breathe life into me so I can see
Do not deny me the peace I seek
For your all the peace I do need

120.
Is there a sun of light?
Behind that shade of clouds?

121. Fantasy World

Fantasy World
Mesmerizing, Dream Inspiring
Mind Controlling

Non-existent worlds on this new found planet
Created by dreams that we've never had
Being seduced by its empty love
Pleasing us with its visible lies
Yet we feed it our souls
While it consumes the mind
Some cheap drug frying our brains
A dictator forcing his propaganda
This fantasy world fulfilling false dreams
Gives us what it says we need
The cyberlord dictating our lives
Making us blind to the true worlds truths

Mind Controlling
Mesmerizing, Dream Inspiring
This is our world

122. What Dreams May Come

Look to the night and imagine a dream
That will bound from star to star
And shoot across the sky in fiery hope
Where everyone will see what you'll become
Oh, what dreams may come

Glance out to the ocean blue
Set a dream out to sail this monstrosity
With sails filled with winds of expectation
Then everyone will see what you've endured
Oh, what dreams may come

Stare into the mysterious wood
Let a dream explore its wonder
The hope of this dream will search you out
Everyone will know who you truly are
Oh, what dreams may come

What dreams may come

123. Lemmings

I looked at the horizon to the new crimson tide
A waterfall fell, flowed like ooze through the night
The stars tried to shine, in the blanketed sky
The smell of this life force makes the lunatic high
Crowds gathered 'round to get a drink from this flood
I watched as they laughed getting as drunk as they could
They gathered around and pushed others in the flow
Laughed while they drowned going down as they would
The lemmings continued to jump in the flood
Sacrificing themselves to this god they don't know
The last of them stood on the shore lapped with blood
And dove in so calmly, while tears filled his eyes

124.
I don't expect the world to see me
I don't expect the world to understand
But I'm sick of living in this worlds' light
And I'm sick of holding the demons hand

So, I'll descend down to my own throne
To take my place amongst the stars
I'll rule with darkness's iron grip
In my name of terror

125. Dark Lord

Dark Lord, he comes tonight
Spanning the star lit sky
Children, to his name cry
Dark Lord, he comes tonight

Seeing a beauty sight
Lusting her be his bride
Wanting to love her right
Dark Lord, he comes tonight

Spearing his heart right through
Causing his fear to see
Killing the love to be
Dark Lord, he comes tonight

Healed he rages war
Capture her as his own
True love gets her released
Dark Lord, he comes tonight

His heart cries to the night
Yet knows that she is free
Alone it feels not right
Dark Lord, he comes tonight

Dark Lord, he comes tonight
Spanning the star lit sky
Children, to his name cry
Dark Lord, he comes tonight

126.
Spitting fire from a sharpened blade
Encrypted with symbols from a holy age
Blindly glistening in the golden sun
The wielder of this white blade knows what comes

Closing a pair of all seeing eyes
To shut out the worlds' unseen terror
The seer now knows what must be done
Time to stand and fight, and not hide

Thrusting the white blade into the air
He sheds tears yet he does not cry
For on this new day a warrior is born
While in the heavens lightning dances with joy

127.
Not one once of beauty has been spared
On the elven princess's grace
It's enough for the sun to rise each morning
It's enough for the moon to shine its light each night
Sadness's tears are dried by her comforting glory
Sorrow's pains flee at her name
Her castle is my temple heart
My life's pulse her magnificent throne
An angels' light is dim to her grace
Darkness is chased out of the corners by her bountiful charm
Consider all of nature's wonders
And everything in heaven above
Nothing compares to her beauty
Because she's a gift from God

128.

Trying to care in this accursed land
Where children's blood runs like soup through sand
Resounding war gong sound of pistol smoke
Destroys the minds simple dream of hope

People kill each other because they can
Bloodlust affecting every woman and man
Taking joy off of others pain
They feed off blood, so they'll remain sane

Violence justifies the every thought
The innocent are the ones caught and shot
They twist the truth till their own demise
And just won't see it till their the one that dies

How can I love in this world of hate?
Where demons sing dance and congregate
A little word with a meaning unknown
Is the world's fuel for its battle drone

How can I love in this world of hate?
Where evil reigns with a devil as its date
Love's power, the world does not know
This power of light the earth does not sow

129.
Humans naturally at one stage were good
But because they are gullible morons
They became perverted by temptation
And became inherently evil

130.

All I know when I'm near you
Is how to be alone
Hang over a pit of pain
Feel so hurt around you
Nothing done on your part
To make such vicious assaults
Just me
Trying to understand
Why when you are gone
My soul calls for you
Yet when the call gets heed
I want to leave
To be nowhere near
Just want to flee
Run from that place
Pushed by my own conscious
From an aura I dare not touch
Fear grips me
Won't let me go
Not till you leave
Does it subside
Then absence raids me
So, I become sorrowed

131.
I can feel it burn in my heart
Fires flare into crevices in my soul
Warm secluded spots no light can touch
Holy hosts of angels near me can't come
A fire from on high has consumed me
Truth in a name burned on my heart
Stars cry out this name
Before the reverence of God
Refining my soul of its hate
All there is, is this light I see
Don't even know what it is to hate myself anymore
Anchor brought me back to life

132.
Drowning in a pool of my emotion
My heart echoes from emptiness
Resounding boom ripples through me
So empty, so cold
I know no warmth
I feel no fulfillness

133.
Bright star on a night nothing dares to shine
Daring even the sun itself
Diamond in an evil world
Bringing happiness to us all
Forever burning in the night
Where daylight is not allowed to blaze
Guiding light to the nations
Inspiring depressed souls
Lead me to a world of joy
Take me away

134. Star

Gaze up into the silken night
And pick a star out from the sky
Watch that light slowly burn
As it casts its glow onto the earth
You wonder how old is this lamp?
For all we know it could be dead
That befell to a possible end
And no one knows at least not yet
Maybe it fell and pulled in space
Along with planets and all around
Or maybe like Little Boys natural father
It seared across in a great bright light
Or maybe yet most beautiful of all
It gave its great life, for something smaller
Something being born in the light of death
A sacrifice so light could continue to shine
Yet this star may not be gone
It's destiny we have yet to see.

135.
Time is a straight line with a beginning and an end ...
But life is a circle with periods of death and rebirth.

136. Freedom

Freedom, freedom, freedom
What is it?
Nothing much obviously
Stuck here
Moping in my own self-pity
Feeling imprisoned by my own emotion
My mind singing to itself
My head molesting my virgin skin
Living eggshell
Trapping life in its yoke of birth
Can't reach out
To break into the sunlight
These four walls
Always drawing nearer
Claustrophobia rips at me
Bleed precious blood
To drown in it only later
Mystical prison of my mind
Can't escape
No hope
No freedom, freedom, freedom ...

137.

See me here
In this constant pain
Nothing to sooth me
Constant pressure crushing me
I know that out there
Someone can stop this
Relieve the crank
And let me free

Take my hand
Lift me to heaven
Lift me away
Walk heavens streets with you
Love of my heart
Mightier than even angels
Ever a servant
Waiting for you to come

War waged on me
Because of you
Endure it all
With knowledge of such love
That's in my heart
Dream of your beautiful face
All the hope and joy it holds
For it saves me from this death

138.

Overpowering presence
Enters into the misty world
So many can't see
So many can't know
Wait patiently shaking
Scared almost
Wondering whether they may come out
Alive with pride
Or maybe this Armageddon and chaos
May elevate them to pitiful shame
Soon the fearful time explodes
Soft screams erupt
Trickle in the belly
Red life falls to earth
One more face dishonorably embarks
To the next life
One by one
Screeches and squeals
Howls to the moon
Furious rage pours forth from hearts
Bent on utter destruction
Betraying friends to defeat an angel
Whose name, whose eerie name
Ever flashes in the minds
From the mouth bubbling forth with hate
While more life lights blink out
Small circle of reincarnation
As no soul may truly die
Not here
In this place where angels stalk
Toying and playing
Ever with the shameful mortals

139.
Why do you
Keep pressing your claws
In my heart
My body slowly dies
As I lose myself
In your life

Gave myself to you
Body mind and soul
Gave away a future for you
Without you near me, not quite whole
Fell in love with you
Threw my gift away
Willing to die for you
Never thanked me in any way

140.

Where am I now
That I have such pain inside
All of my days
Love has just passed me by
Every time I reach out
It seems further away
Such a simple concept
Yet my heart can't handle it
What if I died?
Would love make more sense?
Seeing people not even mourn
What's this life for?
Keep getting passed by
No one seems to see
Me standing here trying
To jump in the tides flow
No one takes me in
What an uncaring world
Find myself drowning
In my and others sorrow
Why do I try?
To catch others eye
Fist is all I seem to deserve
Why do they hate me?
Can't make sense out of this
Feel so alone
No time has been given me
No time for hope
Voice constantly cursing
My very name in hate
Try to set my record straight
Keeps being bent out of proportion
Why do I deserve this?
Why do I try so hard?
Empty void in my heart
So wish to be filled

Even hate cannot fill
Almost knew it'd come here
Lock myself away
In lonely desperation
Crying to sleep
Over destroyed dreams
Dreams I tried to make true
Some ulcer always fumbles
Why?
Why?

141.
Robe of night
Glistens sinisterly in the starlight
Hidden soul
Gently glides over weather beaten asphalt
Soft whisper
Guides him humbly through the night

142.

Saw an apparition
Not that long ago
I didn't want to believe
What it was I didn't know
One thing it wanted
That was to feed off me
It raped it killed
My friends my colleagues
Stripped me of my very pride
Left my soul naked
To the spiritual world
The demons of a darker time
Each different face it consumes
Brings their fury against mine
Harsh and destructive each time
Save me Oh God from this
Ripping me from the inside
Send your angels to save me
Can't trust a pretty face anymore
What demon is inside?
That could once again destroy me?

143.
Marauding hopelessly
Through the endless night
Lives of thousands
Ever on these hands
Stars burning their furious anger
Condemning this damned soul
Horrid monstrosities
Spawned in hell itself
Ever assaulting this frail shell
Wanting to end this quest

144.
Ever watched
By lords of the air
Judging me, testing me
So everything falls to ruin

Trapped animal
Struggling to break these bonds
Despairing cage keeps me down
Howl in fury at my master

The air so stale and stenched
Drowning in products of destruction
Some voice laughs mockingly
Cursing me and damning me

Some days I slip and lose my mind
Want to destroy something beautiful
Ever losing that piece of myself
A circle that sees no end

145.
Cool wind blows over me
Warming my icing skin
Darkened world of warmth
Diseases me to the heart
So why am I here?
Letting myself be so damned
Some voice calling me
Pulling me to this place
Place where I don't belong
Place I do not want to be
Here I am letting the world rip at me
Exposing myself to all this pain
Someone wants me, yet they won't show their face
If you want to feed, then come and suck me
End this misery now
Just do the merciful deed
Let me die with my dignity

146.

Didn't know you loved me this much
To hold me down
Didn't know you loved me this much
To beat me to the ground
Didn't know you loved me this much
To clip my wings
Didn't know you loved me this much
To kill me

All my life I've waited for a break
'Cause of you it's never come to me
Force cold reality on me
Which has killed my dreams
Get away from me
I'm sick of you
I am something, you are nothing
It's killing you; I can see it in your eyes

Such hard love
- Is that what you call it?
Mommy please
- Quite the rude one
Let me dream
- Why don't you just go away

147.
Black night trapped in silken threads
Spreading starlight to those who want to see
Sunken eyes deep within the night
Piercing souls and inner fears

148.

Tainted power flowing through me
Thickens my unscrupulous blood
Causing me to lash out
Molest your feeble soul
Take advantage of your weakness
Why does it feel so good?
Rage is all I can see through these eyes
Hate is all I can feel in this heart
It may be rough, it may hurt
But I no longer care
Because it feels so good
To see you lying there bleeding
Lying there, dying
Now why are you
So pissed off at everyone else?
For doing what I made them do?
Look at me your assailer
I'm the one
You should be raping
Why does it feel so good?
Why does it feel so good?
To screw with you
To mess around with you
To manipulate you
Push your little buttons
Look at me
I'm screwing you up
Now you're so angry
I can see it in your eyes
You wanted my dark truths
Now you know them
Pitiful fool
What did you expect?
A fun-loving puppy
Try a blood thirsty wolf
Why does it feel so good?

Why does it feel so good?
I'm screwing you up
Because I love you
I'm screwing you up
Because I need you
I'm screwing you up
Because I want you
I'm screwing you up
Because I love you

149.

I can feel you
Your name is poison to my soul
I hate you for making me feel
I can go on forever
Don't want an anchor
Just want to go home
Let this boat sink
This battle cruiser has fought its war
Hull battered and broken
Let me sink
Braved my last ocean
You make me go through more
Running out of ammunition
To deal with the pain
I cannot fight much longer
Do not want to see the morning
Let me go under the fluorescent moon
Assail me from under the sea
From above hailing death upon me
Don't want to fight
Just want to go home
Decommission my soul
Let me die, let me die
No more thunder guns rocking me
No more enemies to threaten me
Don't want a name to anchor me
To this punishable life
Don't want you to be responsible
For my pain
Let me sink, let me die

150.

Can you hear my voice calling you?
Reaching out to your humble soul?
Does it scare you; do you fear me?
Stretch my hand out, summon you to me

Come to me, my quiet child
Look past you pain and see this light
It's calling out to you
It wants you

Calling all others

Little voices calling out to us demanding that we purge the world
Insignificant world rebellion wanting to destroy our immortal minds
Enlightened hearts know our truth try to bleed it out of us
We are the ones the holy lunatics that will take back this earth

Can you feel the hate in you?
Nudging you to take up arms and fight?
Do you love it, do you want it?
Stretch out you hand and kill them

Buy back this world with blood, like our almighty Lord
Strike them down, burn their ashes, purge this vermin world

151.
All I know
Is a strong pull by your name
I can feel it
A face in my mind
Corrupts my soul to the point
I can love it
Haunt you and stalk
In my dreams
Where I don't want you
When I see
Your face, you rape me
Molesting
My soul and my mind
All you do is stand there
Love
Slaying me
Driving me to insanity
All because
You invaded my life
Why don't you go away?
You punk
I die each day
I have to see you
A hundred times over
Feel my life pulled from me
Just go away
Go away
Please Lord let me rest
In final peace, take me away
Take me away

152.
Here I am
Waiting for my time to come
For this fantasy of love to come true
Nothing in my life have I begged for more
Then to be wanted
By someone, somewhere
See a beauty dancing in the night
Making herself happy getting off on someone else
Smile anyways, hope to see me
This angel of the night
Lights go low as the music almost stops
Lovers dance to ever easing tunes
Playing my mind
I try to hold her
Falls away from me
To a place not quite close to here
It makes me hurt
To know I'm not in her mind
When she possesses my soul
Gives me an anchor in this life
Drums kick in again
She leaves the room with him
Here I am
Waiting for my time to come
To be wanted
By someone, somewhere

153.

Something in my heart
Makes me feel clogged and stuck
It wreaks sorrow and misery
Causes to fall right down
Emotional collapse forces me to cry
I know it's something inside
Makes me feel alone
Like no one else cares
I feel like I should die
Plague destroying me
This disease unknown how it came
It stole my life
Made me feel empty
Lie around because no one cares
I am dying will anyone cure my pain
The angel in my dreams
Vile of life for me
Remove that clog in place
Fill all the emptiness
Cure my disease
Ease me from this pain
Come and bless me
Come and bless me

154.

Waited for too long
Patiently watching the world
All its sin and corruption
Destroying all the youth
So deliriously brain dead
No one thinks for themselves
My patience is only so thin
Feel the angels screaming at us
Let's get it on
Let's get it moving
Move into the streets
Flood the world with a new voice
Let them know we are alive
Quietly abused
Kill us silently in the night
Crying to the heavens
Waiting for an answer
Lay down here dying
They rape and molest our minds
Sick of all this heresy
Feel the angels screaming at us

155. Can Not Feel

I cannot feel you
I cannot touch you
Your demon star shines in my sky
Dear God, I just want to die
Emotionless soul flung into the void
Lone heart nothing can feel
Bearing memories of horrors old
Spiritual slap you mind will deal
Forgotten dreams still haunt my mind
Star crossed souls dance in the night
My own life I cannot find
Lost under your tyrannical might
Steel hard feelings forgotten
I walk this journey now alone
Secrets into me are beaten
All they see now is a drone
Beat on me and knock me down
Mind's eye can see your soul
Love and care angels are drown
My hate will take its toll
I cannot feel you
I cannot touch you
Your demon star shines in my sky
Dear God, I just want to die

156. Beat Me

As I sleep now, dreaming in my mind
See the ways you molest me
All through the night
Silver blade of pain
Inserts itself in me
Poisons my blackened blood
Then it kills me
I see your face
Haunt me in the stars
Dripping my own blood
Drowning just as I should
Angels do not guide me
Demons like to rape me
Beat me into the ground
Why doesn't your mind see?
Why close your eyes to me?
What is it you don't want to know?
Laugh your curse on to my soul
Just want to hear my cry
Loneliness's pain the burden I must bear
Please stop destroying me
Feel loves pain pollute my heart
No drugs to ease me
Yet I dream of cursed joy
The demon king that slays
Throws me up, bats me down
All I see is your face
In my mind

157. The Prayer

I can see now my power source of pain
I can feel it move my soul
Sorrow grips me from afar
Draws me nearer to the end
Destination of a journey
I have walked for too long
A road of stumbling blocks
I have tripped all too often on
All my mind sees when I look on this life
Is all the hurt this world has inflicted on me
And I pray for the day
That I go to heaven
Love has not given me one once of pity
To relieve all this hate inflicted anguish
I cannot dream happily anymore
Hell freaks are now plaguing me
No light touches me or forgives me
Nothing to bathe me, nothing to sooth me
All these days I have waited
For someone, something to rescue me
I do not know how to smile anymore
What is the point in smiling in the darkness?
Where no one can see the joy I express
No one cares to come down for me
Oh, my Lord just take me away
Away from this place I despise
And I pray for the day
That I go to heaven
And I pray for the day
That I go to paradise

158. Curse

Each day I sit here
Wondering and waiting
For a day when this elusive curse
May relieve itself of me
All my restless nights
Spent dreaming of masked freaks
Images I once knew
Now turned to spoil
Every day I enter this place
To be haunted by the past
Its ghost constantly screaming
The wind whispers this hate
Onto my fragile mind
I lay awake at night
Praying, begging
For this hell to pass me by
Spiritual wars
Of the loved and the hated
Rip at each other in me
Fighting for possession
Of my damned soul
When will peace come?
I'm tired of this conflict
I want it all to end
All the pain all the hate
Take me away from here
Dear God take me away

159. The Damned

Silently awaiting our bloody doom
Holy crusaders raining judgment
Upon us for our masters' sins
Drafted into this hell
Buzzing bombers blasting out paper walls
Flexing ever sickening muscle
To brainwash us with their superiority
Armored warships roaring across the land
Towards this collapsing trench
My comrade lay bleeding
From flying vipers burping forth
Into our accursed flesh
Once masters of our own destiny
World's big brother thought otherwise
Religion I may not necessarily accept
I am assumed to believe
Therefore, they kill me
No wonder I hate them so
Yet they hated me first
For a lie they thought was true
I can't help but think myself a martyr

160. Thief

Shadow men hunt in the night
Through the tall glades of trees
Preying on a fugitive soul
Running from hell
Ominous shapes in the dark
Mask him from fear
Shades strewn across the ground
Betray him to their masters
Running away from condemnation
Due to injustice from on high
The gods are angered with him
For escaping the grave
Killing, raping, hating
They hunt for this dog
Nothing rests while he runs now
Relentless pursuers
They try, try, try to catch him
But he's a thief in the night

161.

No conscious memory
That I can summon for great thoughts of me
Great burdens of sadness
Weigh on my uncertain heart
Salted rivers flow through my soul
Sweeping me away into its fury
When I beach to dry despair
Curl in a ball and try to die
Wanting to fly from this place
Into the blazing refining sun
Burdens of sadness come back to me
Pull me down to the earth
Back into the violent rivers
Eventually again to dry despair
I just want to fly away
Be free from this binding circle
Anchored down by my own regret
Things that happened but I can't remember

162.

Field of empty sorrow
Wind softly blowing through the grass
Insects skitter at the wolfs howl
Eerie velvet sky a navy's hell
Some damned creature stumbling
Through the claw like grass
Grasping at him, pulling him down
Soft cackled laughter emits
As he struggles on
Gasping desperately for forbidden air
Heaves out sweet red life
Feeding, watering the vampiric grass
Heaving out his final breath
Dishonored burial of blowing dust
So the grass can grow him over
His soul becomes one with the earth
Grass sprouts where he once lay
Cackling with the rushing wind

163.
See I am nothing now
Only a specter of my former self
Soft whispers now lonely howls
Attempt to recollect my flesh
Try to touch my world
Spirit shivers till I freeze
Wind wisps my screams away
Voiceless I close my eyes
My skin still real to me
As the shutters descend
Darkness does not ignore me
No longer can I see anything
Grief of loneliness haunts me
Not even angel's care
Everything passes by
My soul is nothing now

164.
Lying here
In a coffin of my own pity
In darkness
Ever dancing upon me
With shadows
Constantly raping me
Lost in a dreamscape
Of my own imagination
Wishing to lose this life
Wishing for ascension to heaven

Your face
Imposed upon these shadows
Haunting me
No peace, not this time
Destroy me
Let me fade from reality
Cross the river from here to there
Of blood and souls along the way
Lost forever in my mind
That live again, in my darkness

Want forgiveness
For all I did, all the pain
Please stop
My body can't take this
Please stop
Something in me still loves you
What did I ever do to you?
To deserve all this punishment
I know you knew it all along
Why do you try to ... kill me?

So tired
Of your stupid deceptions
Scream aloud

As my soul dies
Fly away
From my dreams to reality
Fire surges through my veins
Holy rage lashing out
See myself what I did
No light shines, no light comes
This tunnel ever longer
Keep forcing me
To destroy pieces of myself
Slowly dying through this pain

Why you
All I ever did was love you
Why me
All you ever did was hate me
Dead now
Another part of me has passed away

A Shadow's Cry

165.
Look back on brighter days
So blinded by love
With a heart for the mind
Innocence still mine
Cared so much
Yet blinded by myself
All that's left is ashes
The sun has died
Moon shines holier now
Eerie howl wraps itself
In the streets and highways
The last song sung by grace

166.
Feel alive
In the midst of the death
Pleading mercy
With silence's thousand words
3D illusion bought with blood
Minds can't believe, minds can't perceive
Truth so very sad
Pushing the magnet away
Blasphemous words with twisted faith
Unknown to even this one of us
Unsolvable maze to save this life
The compass has died, leaking its breaths
Lonely beliefs so overwhelming
Sun dehydrates even the dead
Pain electrifies the nerves
Enclosing vice destined to doom
Falling slowly to the cracked earth
Eternal breath slowly fades

167.
Something out there calling me
Hear it screaming
Tries to consume me
Suck me in its claws
Lost the war but still trying
Insignificant flings of life
Can't tame this beast
All these voices calling me
Howling out my name
No one else seems to hear
No one else seems to care
Cry out angry and frustrated
Life pulse is flattening
Wait for it to silence me
As it comes so slowly

168.
Empty void
Starless night
Dim fire
Feels so lonely
The only light now in this life
Created by my own heart
Hollow substance
Barely matters
Nothing cares
Angels can't love
Obsession comes in sweet demise
By a secret my God hides
Careless wanders
Daring ventures
Means little
Heart just fails
Uselessness has stopped the dreams
Spooked silence ever haunting

169.

All I ever needed was to be
The air has just passed through this shell
Sky has been bruised black and blue
Just wanted to be more to you than this one of these
Now the voices have died
Gone deep down inside
Wind reeks with the pain
We're all going insane
Why in the hell did you have to screw me up?
Shoved right where it shouldn't
No more can I pass
Away with this hate
White cloth did I saturate
All these omens I can't find
Cry of you and me so blind

170.
I can never see, I can never touch
I can never smell, I can never hear
I can never be, I can never want
I can never live, I can never die
All I ever knew in you
Was something beautiful
All I ever knew in you
Was something incorruptible

Seems I was wrong ...

171.
Living star
Breathing light on me
Send this curse away
Darkness dooming deep in me
Tentacles choking
Hidden voices laughing
Busy dying
Need something to come

Wash me
Scrub clean the hate
Poison so concentrated
Afflicts my innocence
Eats slowly at dignity
Shamefully hiding
This boiled skin
Cry away the pain

Kill me
Relieve now this place
It's so lonely
Emptiness taking its toll
Sucking at me
Pulling me inside
Resistance in useless
Taking me away

172.
Try to cry
It's hurt me again
Nothings real
Looks so grey once more
Feel the need to be
One with my misery
What's up with this?
Emotions so clogged
As I think of you
Disemboweling my fragile soul
"You couldn't have known"
What I tell myself
The dreams return
Haunt me and rape me again
Emotions flaring
Rage comes hate kills the love
Not again
Watch you run with him
All the pain I feel
Rips at me, feel so cold
Take these memories
As I die, forget me
Want to say
"You meant nothing"
Humbly crying
While I lie to myself
All I needed
Was just a close friend
Why are you killing me?
No, I love you
Why? Damnit!?! Why?
Why me?
Let it end already
Sick of dying
Over and over each time
Let me meet final death

So the resurrection can stop
Don't want to live
If I have to die each day
Stop stabbing me
Let my heart bleed
Don't want to see
You in my dreamless nights
You've burned them all
You're the only one that's left
I just wanna go
Why does it always hurt me?
Let the remedy consume me
Rage out on my body
Here I cry
Its hurt me again
Nothings real
Looks so grey once more
Feel the need to be
One with my misery
Take these memories
As I die, forget me

173.
Unsure silence
All chaos subsides
Nothing stirring
So gently breathing
All so faceless
Fragile skin
Vulnerable in the dark
Consciousness passed to the morn
Lost to selfless dreams
Watchful predators
Keep the herd inline
As she sleeps
This hell turned heaven
Some never quiet
Yet here the stars pass
None notice, none care
Reduced to helplessness
So dependent on these walls
Subtle cold
Never waking
Close those eyes
The dark holds no dreams
None the more special
Uniqueless shadows
Of the waking self
Consumed by darkness
As she sleeps

174.

So many hearts
Enlightening the small room
Joyful smiles in common love
They are one
In every respect
United at the soul

This one heart
Darkening the world
Painful smile trying to love
I am one self
No other invaders
Solitary flesh mind and soul

Don't want to blend with them
Become one with them
See the guilt in their eyes
Prying hearts, lying minds
Don't wanna play their games
To get hurt again
Trying to care
No one cares
Laughing in this misery
Can't see the tears
Can't lose myself

Flesh of my flesh
Blood of my blood
We are one
Turn out the light
So I can't see myself
Don't want to see myself
In what I've become

175.

Precious one
So beautiful to me
It's hard to say I love you
Without actually meaning it
I feel so ashamed
My heart is afraid
Soul screaming for you
Why am I crying?
Sink my vipers in you
To make the pain fade away
Can you tell me you care?
And truly mean it?
Can I look in your eyes?
See the world in a new light
You want me to say how I feel
Live my life in constant denial
It hurts to see you
My loneliness surfacing
Guilt makes me impure
With the things I've done
Forgotten burdens weighing down
Don't think I know love
Yet something pulls at me
Drawing me nearer
Afraid to say anything
Scared of foolishness
Beautiful one
So precious to me
Want to say something
Want to say something

176.

Watching with darkened eyes
At blissful oblivion
The empty hallway
My life's short path
One way out, into the sun
Ever watching, all revealing
Recoiled into shadows
No one cares here
Delaying inevitable death
Amusing my own sorrow
The beat of the music
Ever ringing in my head
Soul based tears drown the eyes
As this brain breaks down
Sprawled on the floor
Staining the carpet with my bleeding spirit
Nothing seems to matter
Save my self-rejection
Lost now to this nights salvation
I await my departure
I await ... it

177. Dead

When I see in your eyes
I knew there's nothing
Where all the dreams and hopes
Of my nights came from is void
Said hello, you didn't even look at me
Passed me by waved your hand, that was it
My first love is dead
I died in her heart, I'm dead
No salvation found in death
Damnation echoes in my head
Let me rot in peace
Suffering in death has just begun

178.
Waiting for it
For the final sleep
Emotions have stopped bleeding
Pulse of hate finally halting
Dreams forever now life
Life's not real, just the fantasy

Till I saw in my dream land
A thousand angels
Around guarding one soul
That looked at me and said ...

Resurrection now
Of this wanting heart
No words can say how I feel
Damnation doesn't seem so sweet
Don't want to be here
(But deep inside I know)
I just want to fly away
(The soul now angel, stole my wings)

Now I see in this darkness
A thousand lights
Illuminating that one precious soul
That looked at me and cried ...

Mind in constant torpor
Living through this unlife
Feel so small and unreal
Refined to tender ashes
Don't want restoration
Want to drown in my misery

Then I was around me
A thousand torches
As that one warmed my soul to life

That looked at me with fire in the eyes ...
Assailed from the skies
Days demons cursing me
In my shadows of sorrows
No sanctuary in this hell
Comforting cries
Ringing in my own head

Then I cry
Unaware of those around me
Down on my knees
Praying under sobbed breaths
For this one angel
Who drives me on

Then I felt around me
Two arms
As the soul wiped my tears away

179.

Hide my face from the sun
Buried in shame, in my grief
Heart cries emotionally burning
Eyes dried from manhood
Speak to shadows of hurt times
To dead friends to my imagination
Frightened words I can't swallow
Yet they're still there
Haunting me

Watch angels close their eyes
Look away so disgusted
Skin shrinks and chokes me
As I scream into the void
Honestly anchoring me
Wrapped in so many lies
Dumbness overcomes my voice
Pray to God for some release
Free me

Feel so small to this disgrace
So afraid of those watchful eyes
Should I open my mind?
Let my conscience run free
Open myself to the world
Let myself again get shot down
All so I can feel free
And come back from this death
For you

Is it worth the sacrifice?
Place the lamb on the alter again
Hand the priest the knife
I know how this will end
Watch you walk away
Just want to feel loved again

No one understands me
Want to open myself
To you

Why am I so afraid?
Simply to be here
You look at me with that smile
My ice melts away
Feel warmth in my heart this once
Makes me feel alive
The one time you were in my arms
That was it, when I felt
I'd die

180. Blue Cheese

Beauty encompassed mind
Screams in my head
Small little regrets of past lives
Hides me from this liberty
Never wanting to commune so near
That pain should replace the fear
Feel so small and ashamed
Watching from afar, too far
Eternal suffering jabs me
No peace descends upon me
My body cries, my eyes drown
Dreams of angels come and go
Everyone else is dead
Can't recall the rest of them
Want to ever dream
Of a small piece of sanity
In this world
Insane, pathetic life
Bumbling chaos spurts forth
Globes, worlds of living pity
What's left of myself crumbles
All that is left is dust

181.

Sitting in the darkness
Where I can't see my face
Shadows engulf me
Hide my fear, pain and shame
Feel the cold tear
Run down my pale whitened skin
Hear my own whispers
As I mourn for my own fate
Await alone here
Not wanting the peoples arms of steel
Just can't comfort myself
So, I wait for the sun's burning rays
God speaks to me
As the sad tunes destroy me

182. Vampyre

Breach the surface
From the uncertain oblivion
Of a dusty coffined grave
Cry in rage to the night
Moon howls
Once it smells this flesh
Wishful predators watch from afar
The soulless keeping away
Afraid of this cold skin
Hear the prayers of children
While I stroll the streets
Of the living
Memories seems so distant
A love that seems so far
Yet so strong
Remember the laughs, the smiles
A magnet that pulled from the heavens
This fallen angel
Heard the prayer of a precious diamond
Love so strong
To pull me back from death
Yet still I am dead
The world so small
What fear do I have?
Since I've seen the other side
The beast roars
As the angels fall for salvation

183. Dark Angelica

Here I am
Freaked and twisted
Light of a hundred candles
Soaked by this madness
Denied and rejected
Socially abused and molested
What light can shine?
Shine on this darkness?
Freak
Fallen from grace
The minds of the herd
Unconditional nothing
A living exception
Breathing corruption on the youth
Reconversion of the soul

No one understands
With closed ears and blocked minds
Dark Angel
Born in darkness
Spreading His light
Guided by a candle
In these shadows
Chilling complexion
As this mortal
Claiming salvation and saint hood
Yet getting nothing

You don't even look
At what the world has done to you
Blame me cuz I'm not like you
Blame it on me, it was me

Possessed by sorrow
Cry in shed of His light
Suffer each day endlessly

The least that can be done
So inconceivable
The pain wrought for thee
Celebrate this misery
Persecuted and dying endlessly
Not much of this earth
Brings joyful smiles
What's wrong with this?
Wanting to be loved
Forged by his fire
So mortally hated

184.

What is there?
I feel so empty
The wind isn't blowing
Yet a current of breath is here
Constantly putting in me
A need I cannot explain
Can something fill me?
What bears the flood key?
Emotions make me lonely
Dear God please complete me
You said you'd always complete me
You said you'd always be here
Soothing my troubled soul
Something's missing
From this utopia
A piece of me is gone
Yet my friends, my family
Are all still here
Torturing my sanity as normal
Dreams constantly depressing
Filling me with angels faces
That are so far away
Don't even see me
Why aren't I just taken away
Nothing is real anymore
Righteous Lord it hurts
Feeling so empty
Shedding tears from the soul
Opening that window as I drown
Said you'd always be with me
I need you now
As no one else is here
Making me an open void and alone

185.
So, this is it
How the story ends
Never ending circle
That has met the end
Of a small instant
Where nothing was real
Emotions that were so strong
Now there's nothing there anymore

It was complicated
How I felt
That I cannot explain
Just know there was something
That made me go on each day
Some small voice in my brain
Made me live, gave me fire

Abandoned I stand here alone
In a place not far from
The realm that I first felt you
But now it's gone
Is there solace anywhere?
Yes, in the reflection
Of the blade I hold

Dear God, let me die
Why keep making me live like this
Every day it pains me
To have to feel this way
The world is empty save me
It's dying around me
Close these eyes and never wake

186.

Look into my eyes
See you dart away
What do you see in me?
At the window of my soul
Where darkness surrounds me
Creating sorrow and misery

I'm not acting
Not in some small drama
Been acting for so many years
Of my pathetic life
I've been lying to myself
Been lying to God

Now I've exposed myself to you
And it frightens, scares you
Do you see in me
A part of yourself?
You lock away, don't want to accept

Became a living shadow
Of the joys in life
Constant sorrowed reminder
Of what life truly is

Look at me I'm a freak
A calloused saddened freak
Can't you accept me as a freak?
God bless the freaks

187. Seraph

So many people say so many things
It hurts me to have to hear their lies
All they see is that which you are not
Something they created in their minds
Because of you people threaten me
Their so shallow and in my heart despised
With the will of an army behind you
Throw out their petty little curses
Nothing but hate from their jealous hearts
When they see, they look at something more
A seraph that dims the stars in the night
Don't dim your light for it guides me
Pulls me through all my hurtful times
It wasn't so much to ask to see your smile
To save me from the abyss of my sorrow
So lost in misery before I met you
Brought an anchor or hope for my sorry life
Pains my soul to see you frown
From all their insignificant curses
You fly higher than them and you know it
Don't be weighed by their spite
Jealousy erupts at diamonds in the rough
At the white roses growing in the thorns
Of all the diamonds you have no flaws
Of all the roses you have no thorns
See them and what they're doing
You're an angel shining bright in everyone's life
Their just mud puddles tormented by furious rain

188.
Awake from my dreams and stare alone in the night
Surrounded in warmth yet I feel so cold
The tears are freezing as they fall out of me
When I see your face in my shadows
I cry out and ask, "Dear God, Why?"
Can't slip back into dreams where all is okay
The world seems so small, so insignificant
While I see you dancing under the sun
Shadows enclose me in my moment of grief
They were at the beginning and now again
Even they can't mend this shattered heart
Feel like I'm dying, losing myself to something larger
Could it be love? Is this what it's all about?
But will I still be alive when my time comes to be saved
Will it bless me this time or slay me again
Hear the lightning blast your name in my heart

189.

Living in my own dementia
Where everything tells me I'm doomed
That I'm more and should not stay here
If I stay here, I'm gonna die
They promised me that
But really is that so bad?
Crouched in my own misery
Where no one hears me but tormenting demons
Feeding my tears with their cursive hate
My heart has stopped beating
This final night screeches through my veins
Clutch my cross as the pain rages
Has the final sleep come?
Will I close my eyes forever now never to wake?
Flare into seizures on the floor
Letting my darkness flow down my face
The voices laugh mockingly their "I told you so's"
Dig my claws in the concrete
As I scream my prayer to the Lord of hosts
Angels look down with pity
Fill my head with chorus's
Fend off the demons raping my flesh
Cry His verses in hopes of relief
Fill my head with Your voice
Tired of being told I'm nothing
Being at the mercy of these wretches
Breathe my last
Fly into the clouds
Attaining the only peace

190.
Watch the angels dancing
On the head of pins
As they dig into me
While I'm dying within
Demons molest my heart
While I'm waiting here
I feel so helpless
How could it end this way?

191.
Bleeding the soul
That water seeds of hate
In the plains of empty sorrow
The world suddenly disintegrates
As the pistol sights draw nigh
On the cold dead skin
Shadows engulf even the light
Mist fogs the pitiful mind

Unable to draw forth
The reapers rapturous beasts
Hounds of screaming death
Can't call upon the cowardice strength
To end my candle's fire
Can't snuff the flame
That shines in the saddened night
Forever to live in this damned state

192.
Why now do I always keep coming here?
Just so despised in a way I've so feared
Everyone laughing in their blasphemous joy
Wishing now, crying here, to be lifted away
Screaming to God, please answer this one plea
Save my enslaved sanity, or in mercy kill me
It stabs me to my core each time I come
Constantly summoned to this durance of hate
Treated like a shadow in the back of their minds
Unless this ghost howled, they wouldn't know I was alive
It sucks and seethes, lives and breathes in me
Any ounce of happiness I may have is stripped away
What is the point of searching for the light?
When the servants are my own worst enemy?
Don't know what to believe of the free salvation
For the price I have paid is the damnation of my soul
Damned forever in this mortal place to misery
Can my feelings ever be free in me?
Condemned forever, since birth on March's Ides
Condemnation, damnation what kind of reality is this salvation
Dance the dances that make me feel like rotten slime
No one approaches me or what I've done for them
Constantly reminded of what I do wrong
I'm nothing but a mistake that keeps screwing up
No one helps me till I'm fallen and dying
Why should I keep putting up with these lies?
Have no skin I've worked it all right down to the bone
But for what, is what I'm asking now
Dear God, why am I worth so little to everyone
Why do they abuse me and keep raping me?

193.
It hurt so bad
So much senseless pain
Accepting
You never accepted
Softly raining everyday
In a land forever consumed by shadows
All that is needed is someone
Anyone
Even before the soft embrace
Life was no ray of sunshine
Looked like you
Acted like you
Yet never liked
Played in all their games
Dying each day
Till the embrace took hold
The black rose
That shines in the night
Sea of blues, whites, reds
So many others
There is no one else
Black tears
Engraved in the skin
Speak silently of the sorrow
Waiting alone in shadows

194.

Feeling so psycho
The angel is stealing my life
A humble Vampire sucking my sanities soul
So hollow now nothing is left of the flesh
Pressing spirit making me lose my mind
Silence driving my heart to the stone
Speech lost to a mind that is so disarrayed
Humble eyes that are drawn to the blinding light
Paralyzed, lost my spine to the void of the dark
Cry out, as I crucify myself this shame
Let my blood flow only to be morale again
Scum of the dirt deserve so much more than I
No mysteries as to why I'm so messed up in the head
Can't even grapple my own emotions to control

Every day I awake to same song of my dreams
Screaming a name I'd much rather not hear
Every breath moving my heart into tears
When will the war chant stop harassing me?
All during this awaken hell reality
I only ever see the same pretty face
Plaguing me like my own bile
Never leaving, getting stronger with time
Eating me alive only to be used as cud
Will I ever live a day without her being part of it
Or is it her unfortunate, damned destiny

Exploring the world of my screwed up reality
Which no one, even me, has dared to wander in
Searching for a cure, answers to my dilemma
Is there a leash to get my inner beast under control?
So that my unsure psychotic soul may rest
Not having to worry about someone else
For I to myself am enough of a chore
Need a remedy to help not remind me of this
Have to stop hell itself from invading again

My world has armageddoned too much already, no not again
Need some peace to calm all the chaos in my life
Look for the eye in middle of the emotional maelstrom

Wound myself to try to ease the pain
Physical torment to ease off the pain of passion
Watch my blood drop slowly in the river of life
Caress the wound in ambers of red hot hate
Don't want to feel this emotion that's destroying my life
While I declare a war on my very own heart
Is there something wrong not wanting to be hurt
That's all experience has taught me about all this
Racking pain as I scream into the sky
Defying the threads of this demented realm
I'm the master, not some dog being led on a leash
Lost control in order to regain myself

Crouch in a corner waiting for my reward
For insolence against my own masters' heart
Fought a war I would never win
Feeling alone is so much worse than death
So empty, just a shell of my former self
Weeping child that lost its way in the world
No guiding hands of parents who helped screw my life
So rejected even angels spit on my corpse
Tied to a car and dragged through the dredges of hate
Insignificantly small that everyone passes me by
When I weep in the middle of the enshrouding night
It echoes back to remind me what I've become
Pitiful whelp drowning in my own tears
This passion's come back; all I see is her face again

Forever psycho she's always in my heart
A burden I carry forever wondering just if she smiled today
The sun burns brighter seeming to mock my disgrace
My concern makes me feel bare right down to the core
Emotionless face doesn't reflect my enthusiastic soul
I can't express the way that I feel I should

Feel like I'm mocking her when I say her name
I'm so insane and it hurts
Like an ice pick shoved through my brain
She doesn't care and I feel uselessly abused
Like a circle it happens again and again
I'm so afraid that I'll never fly in the sky
So, convinced myself that I'm worthless
Treated like a ghost that doesn't exist
Despite my passion for this blessed angelic name
I'm just too afraid of myself anymore
What word can my soul use to say how it feels?
There's only one word I can think but is this love?
I'll keep my ignorance forever and never know
Let her pursue her dreams at the cost of mine
Somehow, I doubt that my hopes mean much anyways
They never have since everyone feeds off me
If what I give up, to see she can smile just once
Is the cost worth this ultimate end?

195. My Gift to You
Walked up the hill
The sun retreating earlier today
Three trees eclipse the sun
As people mourn for the men hanging there
Two are loud and boisterous
Mocking the third
As the mourning barely falls upon him
I look into this man's eyes
The conscious dawns
I know this man
I've seen this man
Darkness rolls in
As the earth rumbles
He looks back at me
Look at my hands covered in blood
Pain in agony flares through me
Depression strikes
Drop to my knees and cry
See his blood dripping from his hands and feet
My guilt overtakes me
I look into his eyes again
Hear a voice "you killed him"
Look back into his eyes
"You killed him"
"You killed my son"
With the nail in my hands
I see the holes in his wrists
"Because of you he's there"
"Because of you he's suffering"
I killed him
He's dying because of me
What have I done?
"He's my gift to you"
Look at his cross and see his name
'King of the Jews'
As he cries

"It is finished!"

196.

There's a reason it had to go down like that
For it's me you see I'm your enemy
My master is the lord of light
I simply live in the shadows which he created
So your abracadabras can't hurt me
Your pitiful curses can't touch me
Thought you knew me?
Obviously, you didn't or you wouldn't have screwed with me
Isn't it plain now, isn't your arrogance real to you
Maybe you should step back, see the world from my shoes
Where not all secrets go unnoticed
So, when you started dissing my work
It was no big deal cuz it's insignificant to me
And I have no doubts you attacked me personally
But we won't get into that
For you assaulted me deeper in my heart
When you mocked my friends and the ones that I love
Had no idea that I cared for them did you
Call them whores in front of the world
Expect me not to get terribly upset
My friends are all that are left of me
When you attack them, you assault all that I am
Jump out of your darkness with you mutated talons
I have no choice but to protect them
And wrap them around with my angel's wings

197.
Engulfed in the inky blackness
All colors are stripped away
True face of all things surface
Blinding invasion recedes away
To leave the candle caressing the night
Raising the seductive pleasures
Desire of the flesh flees
As the false hum of corruption is silenced
No longer poisoning the fragile mind
Soft whispers no longer carried
By the wind of a selfish wanting
In no life span that may satisfy
All satisfactory desires become void
The corrupted flesh demands no more
While the candle burns
Guiding the conscience through darkness
Shines more truth in its humbleness
Then the blinding flash of modern filth
Burns all old desires away
Breathes life on pursuitful passions
Romantic aura so soothing and comforting

198.
What's this I feel in me?
Something's missing so incomplete
Let this hole be filled with these dreams
Filled with the mistress of my heart
Feel so drawn away from here
No thought can sooth that aching place
I'm drowning as the night crawls forth
All I wanted was to see you there
The mistress that consumes my mind
Quench the need to know how you are
See the ray of sunshine in this dark day
The only one that makes me smile this way
Shadow me and stop the sorrowed rain
Falling from the heavens pity on me
Lift me up to the stars again
When the fog clears, I'm here once more
Alone in the shadows feeling that need

199.
Slumbers peace is lost
The night aches on and on
Eyes water from the strain
The tears fall from the soul
The window has opened
Blood taps to the clocks rhythm
Cries of a screaming heart
Resound through me
The sun is rising
Storms of sorrow pound harder
Clouds shatter to the sun
When the seraph is seen
Yet when she leaves
The clouds muster strength enough
To block the sun once more
Each night overcome
With visions of the angel
A magnet draws me
To this place where I don't exist
Each hour praying
That these dreams can break the clouds
Yet nothing comes
No hope or dream
Can replace a seraphs' touch

200.

Sweet voice that flows away
Gentle song with every breath
There's something hypnotic about it
Keeps me wanting to ever listen
Silken lips hum a lullaby
Sooths the soul during a restless night
Carried proudfully with the wind
Nature sings all in tune
With the sweet wind caressing song
Could keep listening
Over and over
Never tiring of it
The voice that calms a storm

201.
Gaping void that runs right through my heart
Me on one side, my emotions dancing on the other
I scream, but no mind hears me
I cry, but no one shares my pain
Lost touch with everything I know I should be
Flailing wildly in my own distress
Can someone save me? Is that an angel I see?
Will someone save me? Make me feel what I need to be

Came to me in my dreams again the other night
Bridging the fatal gap between me and myself
I can feel you right now here beside me
The angel I see in all my dreams
Can you feel my hand as I run it down your face?
Through your hair, you grant me heavens embrace
It's at those times I know that I can fly
Right out of my own misery and into the light
Feels as though I've been brought back to life
Now the dream is real, and I have you here with me

202.

Suck me
What the hell did you expect?
For to me to put up with this
Patience has limits
So does this rage
Tried to keep me down
When I could fly away
Tried to be everything and yet nothing
When would you realize
That I'm better than you

My whole life
You were obsessed with holding me down
In dredges of my own depression
Every time I spoke out
Threw me down
But it's not so fun anymore is it
Stole back control
But you can't handle it
Stole back myself
Been set so free

Forgotten past
I used to be one of you
But unlike you I've been redeemed
Spent so much time hating
I lost sight of the truth
It's so over now
Can't you understand that?
It's time for salvation now
Can't you just go away?
Bleed away my sin

203.
Gone now
Abandoned the ages of damage
It can't touch me anymore
All the demons of my heart
Left them to die in the sun
Where should I go now?
Nothing matters anymore
Where does this road lead?
Nothings real
I'm so lost again

204.
Why are you crying?
You never cared anyways
Always messing with my reality
At every little chance you had
Constantly laughing and scorning
As I ripped my rage filled insides apart
Never realized
What you were doing to me
Every night crying myself to sleep
Your taunting echoing constantly
All these years I've tried
To put it behind me
Now you've gone too far
Forget morality
Apparently you did too
If you didn't hate me
Maybe I would have hated what I've done
Now you're lying there
Bleeding your life
I'm lying there smiling away
Hope I bathed everyone
In my and your blood
As the lightning snapped
And everyone gasped
Even if it's the hard way
I'll teach you all a lesson
We're people too

205.
Echoes of past days keep haunting me
Ghosts of sorrow so unrelenting
This heart has become a tedious burden
Have to carry myself cuz no one will
This life is so helpless
Tears always falling scarring the soul
Was never promised it would be easy
Yet I still pray for release

206.

Can't feel the love
Life has escaped my grasp
The city is burning
The children are crying
Sobs of a thousand voices
Ring through charred streets
Meaninglessness fills the mind
As they ask God why
Crying, demanded to be heard
While the angels watch silently
Mothers embracing their dead sons

The poison reaches my brain
As the shadow flees into the night
Rain is falling stinging the wound
Leak this life into the puddles rings
Lapping back into an open mouth
Hurts to cry, but I can't stop it
Broken and unrepairable
Angel stands there staring at me
Not answering my pleads
Feel so gravely alone
Why doesn't He hear me?

Hey Father
Can't you see me on my knees?
Can't you hear me call your name?
Can't you feel these tears?
Hey Father
Father why?

Hated so much by all I've known
All I've ever believed
Others may feel it
Suffering from the lack of anything
Held down by the hand that feeds

A crying, lonely, abused child
Why can't I just die?
God will never leave me alone
Close these eyes and never wake
Is it really that hard?
Dear God just let me die

Father why?
(Because I love you)
(Because I want you)
Why Father why?
(Stop crying)
(I love you)
(I hear you)
Father why?

207.

Stare into these eyes
What do I see?
No relief, no salvation
Mistaken paradise for hell
Could never have touched the angel within
Unknown death comes back
Unrelenting tormentor from the crypt
Harassing this soul
It doesn't care, it never has
The demonic curse I bear on myself
A thorn placed into me
Reminding me of my humanity
Of my frailty and mortality
These eyes the ever catalyst
Summoning forth the beast
On to this barely coping mind

Reflective eyes
Staring back at me through this blade
Shows me the window into my soul
The one no one but myself
Dares to look through
Rose wounded eyes
Bleeding forth all the pain
Scarring this flesh
The beast laughs at his victory
His cold brutal victory
Draws ever closer
Remember the sparkle of hope
Yet what do they matter
In these eyes
What does it matter if they never loved me anyways?
My flesh screams

208.
The road that lays before me
So quiet and undisturbed
What destinies it holds
Unveiled as our feet slowly trod it
Some fall
As few help to pick them up
The sun reflecting on our faces
What is held in our souls?
Many not knowing why they are here
With the rest of the travelers
Some go to lead the world
In great escapes of reality
Others are there
To simply help those ones
To one day to maybe
Have meant something to someone
And felt something for the person beside them
Or just to have been a friend
To the one who just fell

209.
All I wanted
Was it really worth it
Coping with all this pain
That I always tried to hide
This dream that I went to live
For what I surrendered in my fantasies
Road to heaven
That threw me straight to hell

Can I ever be
Something I wish I created?
Lost everything I was
Will I ever find myself again?

Were all these dreams
Worth the inspiration?
After what they've done
To this sad and pathetic life
Hallucinations come in with grief
Is this escape of a lie
Worse than my harsh reality?
It might just be

Dear God
Never let me sleep again
The pain is so overwhelming
Of what I want and what I have
Are these lies worth these tears?
Price I'd rather pay in blood
Stab my frail subconscious
While crying for what I never had

210.
Where is there freedom
A slave every place I go
Bearing no price
Except the tag of worthlessness
Sold by those I loved

211.

Something was missing
Something that I should have had is gone
What I have been looking for in my life
What I have been needing was stripped away
No more shining stars
In the ungrateful sky above
The sun will no longer rise
As the crying howls will never cease to end

Give me back
What was stolen from me
The one thing I have needed
Apparently is too good for me

Never appreciated
How I felt in my abyssal heart
When the ray of sunlight came down
Jealousy enraging cut me to the ground
Never promised anything
Wasn't given the chance to be promised
Unloving, uncaring, ever hating little harlot
What have I done?
What have I done?

All this sorrow that ever consumed my life
It was time to flip the coin
Time to restart, reboot and be reborn
To heal the scars these tears drove in me
Can never ever be happy
For once in my miserable life
All I ever do is cry
And drown, forever

What have I done to deserve this hate?
The one thing I ever wanted in life
Stolen, ripped, taken away

Can I see past this pain?
To hate you
For what you've done to me
I loved her and I loved you
But now I don't owe you anything

Give me back
What you stole from me
The one thing I have needed
You thought was too good for me
Who do you think you are?
To try to rule and judge my life
Can't trust anyone anymore
Give it back to me

In my mind I've sued you
For what you've driven me to
Total hatred of myself
This worthless waste of bone and skin
Did you want to see me bleed?
Give her back to me
I know why you hate me
Cuz I'm better than you
Cuz I'm better than you

Give me back
This chance to be happy
Give it back to me
Robber of my soul
Give it back

212.

Emptiness
Consumes me
Everyone so uncaring
Hopelessness becomes me
Life is so meaningless
Wreck my vengeance on my flesh
The cold embraces me
Realizations, molesting
Any anchors to this life
Were sailed away long ago
The sun is so mocking
Don't want to see myself
The glass, separating
Not giving into this rage
Can't reach the angel within
Joy an arm's length away
Creating lies to hide me
My heart abandoned
The angels scattered
Hatred comforts me
My terror ever nourishing
This lamb is bleeding
Ever feeding this sorrow
This soul unhealable
Unresurrectable
Yet I'm breathing ...

213.

Rejection is my only friend
I know nothing else
All I've ever loved
Have given me the shoulder
Stare into the starless night
Cuz it never shines anymore
The moon has been shut down
As it bleeds itself on me
Hold this rose in my hand
As it sheds its red
The light escapes my mind
These black pedals are all that are left
I will never again ascend
To what I was never promised
Pride is too good for me
Humbly beating everything I am
The clouds roll their fury on me
Something's in life weren't for me
I'd cry but what good would it do
Since no one is here to hear my sobs
The concrete chaffs my callouses
As I walk away from here
What I've bottled up explodes
Igniting up this nothingness
Not left with anything
To escape to anymore
The beats that once filled me
Have become meaningless whines
Plagues that always haunt me
Constantly freaking on this mind
Precious worthless priceless one
Bear a name that is nothing
Beauty has escaped me
Despicable self that I hate so
Dredge my wounds deeper
Extreme pain helps me cope

Tired of fighting for nothing
But that's all I have left
Try to lose myself in the storm
But the compass refuses to fail
Still forced to deal with myself
The rage this mirror reflects
Compromise my emotions
In the hopes for something real
Tear this crevice in myself
To relieve this flesh of the heart
My mind doesn't need this
Just want to go on living
Don't want to be held down
By something I cannot have
Wishing for better days
In the past when things were different
Where faces that now haunt and taunt me
We're just part of the crowd
That I felt nothing for
Cuz now I find myself here mourning
Over what's stolen from me
Try to fly out from this window
Bleed my soul out on the earth
I just want to be alone
But my soul won't leave me alone
Every time I close my eyes
I imagine myself dying
To escape all this pain
Try to block out everything
That brought me to this place
Each time it gets harder
When I try to cry to God
Wondering if he even hears me
My deafened screams unyielding
Angels in the shadows watch uncaring
As I drown slowly in this cell

214.

Lost control
The river flows from me
Flood gates to my soul have opened
Windows to my fears, out are pouring
Flesh is rained on, drowning
Tried to focus on good things
On the few rays of sunlight
Breaking through these storm clouds
Enlighten my mind with joy
To ease the pain
Damn up the river, take control
Stop it from flooding what's left
Let the water evaporate
Under the joyful sun
Just too much, too fast
No anchor can hold fast
Sweeping away the crafts
No end in sight
Just constantly flowing
As I lay here, crying

215.

You see inside something greater than this
Believed in me when no one else gave a crap
Said I'm better than this, that you were my friend
See these tears as I die all I want is to see you now
Hugged me when I didn't want to live
Made me question all I ever wanted
So weary with my life, my legs won't go on
Never did you give up talking to me
Know when I needed someone right then
Paid careful attention to all my sobs
Even if you didn't care, always listened
Life has so very few precious moments for me
This one I'll be sure to carry in my heart always
Why are you so good to me?
Look at how pathetic I've become
Not even worth your time
But you still hugged me anyways

216.

You see I've fallen, fallen from grace
My misery's brought me here to this place
I can't find my way back home anymore
Clouds block the stars out, veil up the shore
See what I've made myself out to be
Worthless entrapped soul that wants to be free
Dropped to the bottom, rocks puncture my skin
Have nothing to hold too, nothing within
When I cry my sobs drown in the night
Pray and wonder when it'll be alright
Nothing I want more than joy in my life
Relieve all this tension, all of my strife
And I know that hope may come my way
These arms that are open, won't push me away
Fighting these demons to save myself
The hands that guide me provide such help
I don't know where I'd be, if you my friend didn't care
What have I done to deserve this friendship we bear?
I'm a lie, with very little inside to see
You found something inside, deep inside me
What light have you found?
In this monster so downed

217.

Crawled out of my hole
Drawn forth into light
Opened my heart to something
That I did not want to understand
Wait to be wounded again
Along with the rest of the scars
Don't know why I'm not being hurt
Confusion overtakes me
Where has the pain gone?
The only friend that sang me lullaby's
So feeble that it ran off
Loneliness leaves me
The sun is out there shining
Why should I continue to mourn?
What comfort now comes over?
That all I know has ran away
Can't go back to that hole
To where I came from
The sun has pulled me out to save me
Always been my friend
Even when I hid in the shadows
Feel alive for once in my life
Unlike the death I escaped from
Don't know if I can trust the world
But I can always trust
The sun will shine in my darkness
That it will always rise tomorrow
Shine on my soul's darkness
Evaporate the nightmares caught in the catcher
Liberating my sadness
Been pardoned from myself
Been pardoned from pain

218.

Play all of your games
Expecting us to like you
What did you expect?
When you played my fragile heart?
Then moved to the next
Give them a chance
That you never gave me
Now I see through you remorseful lies
So visible now your pitiful mind
Believed in your whacked, created truths
Refused to open your eyes

Run my cold claws down your throat
Tear out your black heart
Feed off your greed, your pride
Never forgetting how pathetic you've become

Demanding all our attention
That we don't want to give you
Why don't you get out of my face?
Spit your name out of my soul
Clip your wings, watch you die
Summon my shadows to strangle your screams
As we delve on new prey
Your flesh has lost its taste
This vampire doesn't want to touch
Sink those teeth in someone else
Watch you yelp in jealousy

Didn't trump on your chance
Now you've euchred yourself
Keep messing yourself up
Get away before you plague me

219.

Step it up cut me up
Drink my blood
Show no mercy
Dance on my grave
What is left of myself
Could never be touched anyways
Been wasted to the bone
These charred remains
The only dead testimony
To what I was
Yell at me for what I'm not
Bite back your lies
What is left is too messed up
I could never care anymore
Too much pain has numbed me
Your pointless rants are not even mocking
Make me smile at your shame
My death has ushered in new demons
The ones I control
This new terror is my hope
Your fear of what I am feeds me
My rebirth has come
What's resurrected is not the same
The light has left me
That you had put into my soul
I've been released, redeemed
Your bonds no longer holding me
No longer puppeted in your delusional games
Closed my mind to your lies

220. Love Song of the Unforgiven II

Walk this road
Unknown where it goes
I can't go back there
To the place I belong
Spread to much hate
Angered too many to count
Lost the meaning to everything in life
When I turned my back on the dawn
Embraced myself to the night
Surrendered to damnation
Sweet taste of bitter life
Has left my chapped lips
Can't even remember who I am
Destroyed myself to create this lie
Everything gone away to the horizon
Fled to heaven, and driven me to hell
There's no solace in my mind
Subtle tranquility turned to chaos
No longer can I escape to the dreamland
My sin haunts even my subconscious
It has plagued my fantasies
Can't hold on to anything anymore
Everything falls away in the end
I can't change what I've done
Or warm my cold subconscious
This place only keeps to hold me down
Tried to say I never cared
But I cared too much
The road is lonely
But I leave in hopes for tomorrow
Until I forgive myself
I can't come back
Don't want to leave here
All I've come to love
Can't keep this curse on them
That burden is just too great

The answer lies beyond the next horizon
I can't turn back
I want to turn back
Though I have one thing
One thing in this place
Left to believe in
For that reason, I may come back
Bur for now
The belief drives me on
To find solace and forgiveness
So that the burden I am
Will be lifted

221.
No escaping the pain inside
The capping sound so far off
Gentle slash and drops of blood
Too far gone, the release has dimmed
So many people wanting too many expectations
All these hopes placed on me from on high
Beaten down, don't understand all this
Lost in the storm of my own confusion
What I want, what I get, so different
Yet all watch, make sure I'll stay alive
Neglection and acceptance
So alone yet everyone says they're there
Yet my heart is dying
Want to run away, leave no anchors
Drift away to a place of forgotten memories
Never remember myself or what I've become
Let myself brew in what I've left behind
It'd be better that way
No one else seems to agree
Yet I feel such pain
Why can't I have abandoned myself
And hope to let the thoughts pass
To reconstruct myself into something better
I've tried so hard to not be this
Which I'm told I'm not
Don't want to deal with this
That's why now I cry
Let the hurt leak
Maybe someone will see
Just so tired
And I want is to go home
Sick of travelling this journey
Don't want to keep walking to the next horizon
Want to fly away
But my wings have been stolen
No one wants me to leave

Taken away my escape, my freedom
Can never really move on
For even if I betrayed them
I would just come back in the end
The guilt too much to bear
Return to this place I don't belong or want
Just want to say goodbye
So I can finally pass away
Uncurse everything I know
So I can stop playing with my mind
Like everything else in life
But the escape is so far away

222.
I've resisted
Freed from bondage
Deliberation
Of my destruction
I'm jaded
Of this plague that's killing
Life
Vacant dreamscape
No more hope for the future
Angels have purged my subconscious
Painless, uncaring
I am resistant
The portrait
Shatters
No more blueprinted guidelines
Nothing is left
That I want
Nothing
Except this absence
Of what I
Used to be proud of
Laughing
I have resisted
It's wasted
Temptations, molesting
Trying to break me
That flesh
Caressing
Wanking emotions
I cannot
Take this
Resilience cracking
Breaking, leaking
I'm dying
Yet I
I

I am resisting
Price of this glory
Worthlessness
So undeserving
What have I done?
Confront this
Release me
Just please release me
Scrape off the tension
Blasphemise my obsessions
Take them under
Forever
I have resisted
Forget you
I have resisted
The urge
To end
Existence
I have resisted
Believing in your lies
Never judging
Your mind
Don't judge me
Don't make me
Your lie
For I
I have
Gone and resisted
Pollution
Already despising
Painfully coping
With nothing
Dune wastes
Chaff me
Hear it
Calling
Too many starless nights
Left wandering

Wandering
It beats me
Feeds me
All this hate
What am I?
Who am I?
I won't surrender
Won't give in
Stubborn refusal
To become one
With greed
Though the light
Has left me
Want to see
My tomorrow
I won't take this
I won't accept this
I have resisted
Stronger now
Skin hardened
I can bear tomorrow
I
Have
Resisted

223.

Can't reach my hand out
Not sure about this anymore
Tried so hard, got so far
Destroy myself
To not infest the clean
This poison and misery
Crying the nights away
In blissful pain
Have a perfect angel's ear
Where all I do is mourn
Joy is my rage
As I never feel it anymore
I scream in fury
She stands there unwavering
Never stops relenting
To hear my pain
Softly comforts my sobs
Arms vice me
Ice the fired demon
My mind being raped by myself
In what I want, could never say anything
What's in this heart
For the perfection before me?
Why I'm still here?
Of the reason I haven't left this hell
Jab the knife into myself again
Rehurt myself so I don't feel this
But it just comes back to me in the end
I know it will
Spotless and clean
So beautiful and pure
Could never bring myself
To mark with corruption
A piece of blackness
Doesn't deserve that
I could never forgive myself

I can't even forgive myself
For what I've done already
Been so good to me
Feel as though I've taken advantage
Of that purity
I'm just such a disappointment
A mortal mistake
Should never have lived
All those years ago
Cuz now I'm here
Putting tiny impurities
In the jewel of the night
Maybe she can forgive me
But I can't
I'm not good enough even for myself
Goodbye sweet angel
This unworthiness is fading

224.

This new night falls
The wolf howls to the moon
The new dawn of misery arises
All wonders aroused
Could this be it?
An ending that we all await
Old rain drips from the troughs
Arousing anticipation
Cold shivers haunting
Eyes blinded by lies
We'd rather all believe
Mist descends to reclaim its birthright
To encompass the flesh we bear
Takes us away to a better place
Where we no longer can die
Sorrows of our past become lies
Angels hug us, call us 'friend'
Become free from our pain
No longer carrying our guilt
Of what we try to drag with us
Love embraces us like a blanket
Not being denied of this right
Revisit those we've lost
Those we've loved through time
Taken away to a better place
I never want to go back home
To the earth consumed in hate
Here I can feel the love
I can feel the love

225.
Empty
Alone
Crying inside
For the tears outside this shell
Have dried so long ago
Smiles
So fake
No happiness here
Only momentary joy
That escapes me
When all have gone away
Want so much to hear someone
To know that I am not alone
I hear the voices
Of all the drones outside my window
Yet still I yearn for a softer voice
The friendly one that comes in the night
That comforts me when I'm down
It falls away from me
Wondering why
The angel's whispers
Consume my needs
The only thing I want
That keeps from the land
Where darkness falls forever
Where no man even wakes
The ballroom of demons
Ever dancing
Yet I fall not to this realm
Managed somehow to save myself
With the need
That pulls at me
Draws me closer to some other place
Let my mind swim
In the gentle wind
That comes when I wish for nothing more

To feel something for once
Touch this uncharted heart
Moves me in a way
I cannot ever understand
Lay here waiting for tomorrow
So different than yesterday
When I wanted to sleep
Forever
Yet something came to me in that moment
When the final stroke was all that was left
It saved me
Basked me in forgiveness
Let me know it was all alright
Fearing I may never hear such a thing again
That it was the only time it would save me
Don't want to let go of that sweet sound
The only one I wish for more in my life
It depresses me
When the silence returns
To wait again
What seems like forever
When the night falls
All escapes to havens
Even the hopes of tomorrow
The time drags on
Peaceful sleep never falling
Grace leaves me
The only thing I had left to hold onto
The fight for escape
Consumes the every second
Till my mind is freed
To the dreamscape
Of my shattered subconscious
Where my needs still aren't met
See the lips moving
Even hear the breaths
Between the words
But it's not enough

Even if I were to hear the sweet music
It still isn't real
My mind can't cope with what is fake
All I see is flesh
Want to hear that fleshes soul
The dream turns to hell
When I wake and find myself alone
The dark mocks me
Absorbing my sobs
Wait till the sun breaks the sky
Wait through the turmoiled day
Not hearing anything
Unattuned to the laughter
That is directed at nothing
Can't partake in that joy
In that orgy of shameful bliss
Source of joy is gone
Never coming near
Search reality for an answer
To hear that something
Come back to me
Hunt in my soul for a solution
Find myself treading a worn path
To reach to edges of the world
In the soupy hell
Of what consumes us
In that which marks
Everything we mark towards our hate
Plunging myself into it
To hear once more
The sound of perfect music
Risking myself
From the maelstrom of friendly rage
Jealousy I must evade
Of those that wish to take away from me
What my soul has always wanted
It knows this all too well
And unknowingly seeks to take this gift away

All the times I manage to lift the callouses
And shed these tears
When my soul breaks
Under this tension
The burdens dig in so deep
Can't help but cry
Here alone
With no comfort, no security
No guarantees anymore
The pains too condescending
That I push to the end
The bitter end
It's the sweetest sound
That always pulls me back
That allows me to see what I've done
To open my eyes
Hold me accountable
For what I've done
Instead of hiding it away
Instead of dying
I breathe another
Let it seethe in me
So I feel alive again
Hearing sweetly
Ever sweetly
All I ever wanted

226.
Reach out, grab hold
Of a hand, I should never grasp
Drag me, up from
The pits of my insanity
Subtle accountability
Placed on me
Stretch for hope
Feeding me
With sovereign light
Uncertain of what's going on
Something is moving
Been revived
Something's different this time
Life has replaced this death
Fire has replaced this ice
Sun shines once again
Don't understand
Why reach into the shadows
Where nothing makes sense
Into the confusion
Figure something out of this
Breathe light
Into my mind
Been freed from this prison

227.
Gentle voice so haunted
Fresh tears still cry from her lips
Ever mourning for this
It strikes me, it hurts me
Sorrow ever consuming both of us
You cry, you die
Seeing the misery she's going through
The world has never stopped relenting
Just wish there was something I could do
Besides sit here and cry
Mind wanders to thoughts of you
Weeping again this time
My heart falls
Below the state of my old sorrow
I feel so helpless
Unuseful
What can I do?
What can I say?
Please God help me
Please God help her

228.
Here on my knees
Crying for new salvation
Not my own
Something drew me here
To plead for protection
To ask God to come to earth
Somewhere out there
He was needed, he told me
Drove me to my knees
So His power could be made seen
Didn't know what I was doing
Choked on the tears as they drown me
Offered them up as my testimony
Of what is in my heart
Begged with my hands held high
For the angels to come
Someone was out there
That was in my heart
Needing and searching
Never really cared this much before
Find myself asking why
Being the second time I came before Him
About this same one
This one that is in me
The worry consuming
Cry the prayers in my concern
Trying to say how I feel
Find myself mumbling unable to come to
Explain what my heart feels
It's all so confusing
Why am I here doing this
I thought it was over
Fortunately, that isn't true
Cuz now I'm here again
Pulled back to this agony
Never imagined it mattered this much to me

But these feelings do
Arms of peace hug me
As the Lord assures me I'm ok
This hearts cry, won't go in vain

229. The Escape

Looking up
Crying out for nothing
Lying my way to innocence
Avoiding cold inevitability
Of silence abounding
Knocking the thoughts in my head
The need to scream
Pain so contagious
It has infected my soul
Reflection of this worry
Still haunts me like demons
Can't run away
All I can do is cry

Remember the weekend
Passed off to the next bottle
Escaping for the time
Away from all these realities
Drown it away, forget about today
Forget about this crap that cries here
For this contagious pain
Sorrow sucks me in
Back to a place where I belong
Didn't want to come back here
But it wasn't an option
Paid the price for your joy
I could have been happy this day
Surrendered it off
To be a testament of what I am

Keep running away
So you can lose yourself again
Let go of your control
Don't believe you have it anyways
What is in that void that is so comforting?
What has this god offered you?

Where is this freedom?
The taste so addictive
The maiden should offer yourself
To this blood each week's night

Is there no solace
When I think of you
In your escape
It scares me
To the point I want to run away
Back to my own pain
Where my blood ran cold
Pain replaced this hate
Emotions were killed
I cry alone
Thinking of you

Fall to my knees praying
For I don't know what
And I stab myself
Again I don't know for what

230. The Black Widow

Every time I look in your eyes
I see the truth in what I am
Rejection in the sparkle
Never really belonged in this plane
Reality shatters, the razor pieces slice me
More marks in my flesh
Never really anything to anyone
I walk through each day praying

Worthless

Never hear the voices chanting in the night
The phone never rings and comforts me
Black widow spoke to me the other night
Offered me her bite if I said the final 'screw it'
Remember all the pain this world put me through
Stretched out my arm, let her climb it up
Till she grasped my neck and licked it tenderly
Dear God just let me die tonight

The world doesn't want me
So the widow said
I'm nothing in anyone's mind
As I was locked down in my subconscious
And lost control of my reality
My head buzzed, ever dying, ever crying
Set myself free from all of this
As she kissed me, and I slept

I'm worthless no one wants me
They all reject me like I'm nothing
Accuse me of not being your friend
But you were never one to me either
You're my precious friend and I love you
But your friendship makes no sense to me
I see it in your eyes, in your face

Play dirt with my enemies, expect me not to see
Worthless

So, I run
Down the street's hard rain
To melt the hurt away
As it burns in me, my hate
The banshee screams as I plunge myself forth
Never caring about myself
The pain lets me escape my heart
Guilty watch blindly as I bleed

231. Wasted Life

Sitting here alone
Yet not feeling anything
Thinking of you
Brings me painless hurt
I feel I should be crying
That my heart should be dying
Uncertainty overtakes me
Guilt starts to rack up inside
I just don't care anymore
This whole life is wasted

Spent my time, those sleepless nights
To imagine a perfect world
Where the sun always shone
With you in my arms
Something shatters this reality
The shards cut into me
Replaced with visions of my own death
Embracing them so tenderly
I just don't care anymore
This stupid life is wasted

Maybe it was a mistake
To hold on to love
To hope for something more
To believe in empty promises
It can't be this way
My soul has died, my heart is wasted
Yet I still love you
Though I try not to

I just don't care anymore
Drive down these rainy streets
Going nowhere, it doesn't matter
Hammer the engine, screaming at me
As we fly through infinite

Escaping forever
Why should I care?
This useless life is wasted

232. Homefront

Reality so disturbed
Nothing worth remembering
Songs with a thousand uncaring souls
The stairways never ending
The bruises never unswelling
Emotional cutting, still bleeding
Crying at night, so seething
Never really knew salvation
Holy ones despised me
Is there any hope beyond this pain?

Something is moving through the river
Is it good enough to be real?
It's igniting their hearts, re-moving everyone
Revival is spreading

Darkness so corrupting
Stole away my innocence
Left me nothing to live for
Accused me of something I never was
It killed me, so harshly
Left me by the wayside
They haunted me forever
Even after the hate
Barely coping
Is there any hope beyond this pain?

He's moving the people
That don't even know him
To love me
And show me himself
The Son is rising
The holy no longer ashamed
He's a spreading brush fire
He's shining
Intoxication is dropping, the bottle shattering

Strange mists are venting
Songs of our hearts are louden than ever
Angels have joined in our chorus
Show them the baby and His tree
The tough start crying

He's moving
A gateway that's changing the world
This dark and uncaring world
It breaks me
Down to my knees crying
I love Him, and I forgive them
We've reclaimed this thresh-hold
He's moving

233.
Welcome to my earth
My world that is my own
Everything that is built is by my hand
I am the creator of this realm
You will never take away
This misinterpreted utopia
I've breathed life into the air
This world is mine
Rain down in the night
Light the skies with fire
You will feel my frustration
As you burn in your havens
Blocking the stars out
Erupting your invasion
Belch your lies on me
My world will take you

Bring it on
You will feel my rage
I won't let you in
You could have tried asking
Before forcing yourself on me
Never mind your army
And your uncertain salvation
You will never destroy me

Missiles screaming
Consuming your weak children
Fires burst out as we scorch the earth
To leave nothing worth taking
Bullets fly right into your skin
Exploding your offspring
We will fight to the end
No matter the outnumbered odds
You won't take us alive
Forget your deceptions

Forget your lies
Forget you and your people

Give it up now
We won't give in
You won't win
I am not defeatable

234.
My scars bleed from the ages of pain
A crying spirit that mourns for this world
The hurt consumes me, plagues me
Surfaces all the weaknesses, ever haunting

235.
Cast away from the sight of watchful man
I feel the rejection of your mocking words
Never accepted into anything except hate
Why don't you kill me and end this charade?
I can still hear the voices that brought me down
The faces are in my dreams when I close my eyes
You can never look in my eyes honestly
And tell me what you really think of me

236.

I've run away, because I'm scared of you
I've denied myself, because I hate my life
Tried so hard, to be more than this
Could never find any true solace in this place
Hidden away, from life, from light
Screaming heart wants release, can it ever come to me?
Always been afraid of all of you
Feel so small, like I'm nothing true
Wanted to save myself, but the sky never opened
This light in my life, says 'it'll be alright'
Can't believe someone cares about me
Rejection is all I have left

The night's cold, eats at my dying flesh
As I run, run frenzied from my fear
My heart possessed by self-imposed damnation
Something pressures me, and breaks me down

237. Mommy and Daddy

And I scream
My lungs rage out this noise
Everyone stuck in their own delirium
Pass me by without a second thought
They all came for me when I wanted to die
Now I'm dead and no one cares

Had come upstairs needing someone's ear
My father was sleeping, never really listens anyways
Just nods his "mm hmm"'s to everything I say
I know he loves me, but I don't feel it
My mother is lost in cyber space
Forgetting about real people that need her
Her business now something that can never be touched
Touch of one key and it could all be gone

Both lost in their worlds
Both more concerned about themselves
Feel like I was never born
That I'm no one's flesh

Where have I gone wrong?
When did I become this mistake?

238. The Family

Surviving, something I'd rather not do
Almost falling victim to my own hand
The wishes still on my mind
To see His glorious face and find peace
Not supposed to ask questions
But I want to ask Him personally, why

Found solace, in the midst of the chaos
Among the other rejects, not wanted
The scorned, the mocked, the animals
Never judged me, just accepted
To run away from those that rebuke me
The ones that are supposed to be family

I can feel their eyes, watching me
I can feel their faces, mocking me
I can feel their hands, beating me
Can this salvation rescue me?

My family I'm not like them
The siblings all don't understand me
Tried to tell them but some won't listen
Don't wanna listen to my nonsense
This blasphemous garbage is worthless
Run to escape this oppression

I've been through hell in my time
I've seen the dark side no one sees
Witnessed the hate, felt the pain
Everyone treats me like I'm artificial
If that's true
Why are these tears so real?

Say I've got something to offer
Got nothing but my dead heart
These tears are all I put out

No one wants to see them
No one wants to hear them
My family, my brothers and sisters
I love you
And I know, I hope, that you love me
But I can't feel it
And there's sometimes I hafta make myself believe it
Even when I'm in one of your arms
There are still days that I want to die
That I wish my hand had succeeded

Angels surrounding me
Their arms ever around me
As I wait for the next time
As I wait for the new tears

I can feel your eyes, watching me
I can feel your faces, mocking me
I can feel your hands, beating me
Can this salvation rescue me?

Father save me
Please Father, please
Can't give up on your promise
You said everything would be ok
Please Father, make everything ok
Scare away the monsters under my bed
So that my brothers and sisters,
Don't hafta hear me scream at night
Do the family a favor

239.
Try to love nothing, yet I cry for everything
Close my eyes for something to let it be meaningless
Stab myself to kill my heart, bleed out the emotion
As my spirit fights this war against my mind
No one sees the pain I fight each day in life
Hold out my hand its shot away, left to lick my wounds again
Just let it bleed and let angels carry me off
To see my maker so he can judge me and let me die
Can never hope for salvation in this life
Take away tomorrow to escape the next tear
Please God, I love you, come and save me
I have nothing left here to live for
Why make me continue to live through this hatred
Lift me the suffering of the new dawn

240.
Cold air ate away at me in the middle of nowhere
Home so far away, lost to the mind
In the midst of the corruption that slew me
I faced down my demons so I could wake for the dawn
The new light so far off, sleep evading my eyes
Lay frozen in my pain and tried to ward off the hell
Gone to a haven, that should be forsaken
Finding solace in a place I should not be
Lost myself to a new star, though I couldn't see the sky
Sorrow escapes my soul, joy invades everything

241.

Living God
Rescue me from myself
Cuz I know
I can't do this alone
I tried and fell
Tumbling aimlessly through the night
Waited for a time to die
To end the cycle, to end the pain
I waited for the tunnel to appear before me
So I could approach the light
But You had other plans for me
And denied me from destroying myself
No matter how much I stood there and cried
No matter how much I asked You to let me die
But You showed me a light
I screamed for help and for mercy
As these old wings I had clipped
Sprung back to life
I was foolish to think I could handle myself
That life was a free ride
But it wasn't free, it had a great cost
A fee that You gave me the money for
But I took it a little too late
Too late to fix my hurts and pains
But just in time to recreate my emotions
To pick myself up again
Realize now I can't stand alone
This house will never be divided again
Together we stand, apart I fall
Be with me always
Never let me leave You again
My friend, companion and king
Help me to keep You in my sights
I never want to be alone again
Living God
Rescue me from myself

Cuz I know
I can't do this alone

242.

Release me from this state
I can't even force these words out
My heart doesn't sing to me anymore
Can't hear the cries of a healing soul

And I wonder what happened
All this joy is coming at me
And my words can't come back to me
I'm chocking as I try to sing to the world
Just stand here in silence
Waiting for God to speak to me
So I can reach out again
Without my common negativity
Instead, I want to sing of new things
Of all those wonders I have refound
I wanna sing of love, abounding
And of the greatness of this world
I wanna sing of God's unyielding mercy
As he pulled me back from damnation
I wanna sing of the times
That heaven embraces me
Just for those few moments
But I can't think of words to say
These emotions are just too insane
Even this song can't express them right

When I look back at what I've sung now
I see the release had come to me for now
How long will I keep this?
Dear God let me keep hearing you
Speak to my heart

243.
The shot rang
As the cold rain falls on me
My flesh not breathing
Carrier of life, leaking out
Littering the asphalt
Pray for the angel to hold me
But she's so far away
Want to feel her warmth
For the last time
Before I fall away from here

Because I'm leaving
The heavens are opening
I'm not coming back from this place
I've been called home
But I'll wait at the gates of heaven
Won't live through paradise without ...

The city of gold
Was so beautiful
The pearl gates, so wonderful
I could hear God calling me
To come to the place he prepared
When I looked down and saw you
Crying over my grave
'Dear God, I love you
'I want to be with you
'But as long as my love is hurting
'I can never partake in paradise
'As long as the other half of my life
'Is burdened in sorrow
'I could never live'

'I'll wait here
'At the gates to paradise
'Till someday I'll see her walking down the path

'I'll sing your songs till that day comes
'I'll wait at the gates of heaven
'Won't live through paradise without her'

244.

Fill me, release me, reach down to save me
My blood flows from my veins
Feel all the rage and all the pain
I could never escape this hole
The world is eating me and inside I'm dying
I feel the faces looking down on me
Judging me, condemning me
Who are you? What right do you have?
I've been sanctified and been made holy
Get outta my face, I don't need you
You and your worldly lies, you try to deconstruct me
But do you remember what lives inside me?
Don't tempt me, don't push me
Could never understand what it is that's made me
Even as you poke me and prod me
He tells me not to retaliate for vengeance is his
And I laugh, because they have no clue

245.
I couldn't drown in my sorrow
I had to die
I couldn't marinate in my tears
I had to die
I was just left here
To face life's trials alone
In the hours before the day of the sun
I had to die

246.
I reach out my hand
As the legions of defeated Hades assail me
Crying out your holy name
Feeling your spirit move through me
To push back the unforgiven warriors
They break like the brittle grass they are
Unable to come close to me anymore
I hear the demons scream in frustration
I hear my enemies wail in anger
As my heart sings praises to you
I am an army of one
The only weapon I bear is your name
For with it I can tear down any barrier
No fortress may stand before me
The stumbling blocks on my path smoothen
The mountains of trouble provide a pass
Nothing can stand before me
For you Lord protect me with your arms
I can feel your presence and your spirit
You've given me wings to pick myself up
So that I can make your light shine
In the midst of the ever-present night
All the nights that I've spent crying
Your love was always there to speak to me in the end
Even though I have nearly descended to the grave
You have made me stronger than ever
And though the dark foe avenges his defeat
I know you will pull me through
That you will send your angels to guard me
By your name, the shadows obey my commands
And I will cast them out to the light
And make them accountable to that light
So that they may know the truth
With your law on my heart, and your name on my lips
Lord, I am an army of one

247.

Fell away to the dreamland
Led away by the Sandman
His dust invading my subconscious
Making my dreams begin to breathe
The night stretches on as I escape
No end in sight yet
Nothing to stop me from dreaming
Nothing to stop me from becoming
I'll just keep walking this path
So I don't have to feel anything
Till I find myself walking, walking
Am I awake, is this for real
And I see her standing beside me
Talking with me, singing her songs
Laughing away with my company
Hug her, feel her heart beating
Wherever I am now
Whisk me away to that place
I don't wanna leave
Cuz when I wake it all falls away
And all I'm left with is myself
I don't want to face this day alone
Not after what I've just been shown
I can't imagine what it was all about
As I try to make sense of it all
Denied the understanding
Left with a disastrous mess
I could never hope to sort anything
My mind is so doused with delirium
Come, Sandman, take me away again
So I can feel her arms around me
And feel true love surround me
Plead with God to allow this to come back
It's the only hope I have

248.
Reawakened memories of feeling I thought I lost
Resurging the flood of tears that should have dried up
Losing faith in myself again I look up to the sky
I listen to the words of the faithful's music
Trying to find comfort in holiness
Nothing is working, Lord, nothing
I don't want to be alone right now
But no one is out there listening to my screams
All I want is to talk to someone that's in my heart
But I can't accept that my words will mean much
I'm reminded of the time I tried to steal my life away
When I just about left everyone in this place
My pride in myself was bubbling over
I thought I had the right to take life in my own hands
And now I'm scared because I feel so alone
I want to be hugged by someone out there
To feel the kiss of a rose on my brain
These tears are the only thing that come to me
As my enemies' poke at me once more
What are they trying to make me do again
I'm afraid of what I'll be pushed too
Help me Lord I can feel I'm falling
Don't leave me alone right now
Send someone that can talk to me
Cuz I hurt so bad inside right now
Even though I feel like running away
I know that those are demons trying to force me away
What are they scared of that they should torment me
I am nothing, I am pathetic, and I am weak
Groveling in my pity as I ask for someone's touch
I just want to run away, but I know that it's not you pushing me
Let me be at peace, I just want to cry
Will these tears water the seeds of hope?
Or nourish a flourishing plant that's already bearing fruit?
If so, I can't conceive it
But that is because of my own human failings

All I want right now is to be near a child of yours
Someone who can comfort me the way I need
Even though you are with me always
It's hard to have to face down the darkness without a child here
As much as I cry to you
I just want to hear someone praying with me
Rescue me, send me a buoy to help me float
Cuz I'm drowning Lord
This is going to be a long night I know
But give me a chance to be comforted at least once
By the child that I want to be near now
Help me
Lord
Help me

249.

The cry of the nations, as they plead for salvation
We march through these broken streets
With swords on our tongues, though the battle is won
Yet we face all these trials and temptations
And we'll make our way through every alley and street
Till we've brought peace to everyone

We're going home

250.
Flying through the space time
Nothing to stop me
No one knows where I am
The wind rushes in to chill me
As I feel my cold heart racing
Can't outrun the storm
Each stop I make it catches up
Can't escape the monster
The window can't block it out
As it reaches in to chock my mind

251.

I don't want the sun to come out and shine on me
Cuz it's only a symbol of a soon coming misery
All I wanted in this life was to be truthfully happy
But I can't imagine if this is what it's ever gonna be
Feel the rage pulse through me like new blood
It gives me life, satisfies my every urge with screams
Using adrenaline to forget about anything, everything
Feeling empowered by something outside myself
Is this the only friend of mine that I can keep with me?
It always makes me feel as good as I want to be

Die everyone who doesn't care about me or my body
Die everyone who doesn't care about me out of body
Die everyone, shoot me in the back while I run away
Die everyone, cuz I don't care anymore

252.

Your artificial I can see through your lies
You wanna play my heart, well I'll mess with your mind
Die
Worship your gods who don't give a damn
Look away as your claws destroy me
Die
Not some toy you throw away in the end
Worth more than that, yet you play me
Die
Write your words that echo aimlessly through the night
That'll find another poor sucker and pollute him
Die
Hard to believe that you could do this
Even your beauty has its ends

253.
Silence presses on me
Stare into all your eyes
Think you know everything
Everything is feeble lies
Fabricate your minds
To what you think I should be
Don't try to mold me
It'll only drive you insane
When I break your casts
All illusions will fall away
I am nothing
Of what you thought I should be
Why don't you open your minds?
Let my expression be free
Too busy sorting everything in my life
To play your roles, to play your games

254.

Heal my broken spirit
Submersion was your command
I went to the water and drank
I let my spirit be cleansed
Let all my sin be washed away
My youthful spirit of honesty still with me

Yet that was so long ago
Now I pray that as I come back to this water
That you will bless me
In my honesty forgive me for my calamity
To let the suffering be washed away
Let the slate be clean
The marks that plague my skin be wisped away
Let me drink once more
Give me your wisdom Lord
During these periods of attacks
That the devil has burdened me with
Harsh reality was used to try to kill me
But I grasped your hand once again
And called on your name
The legions of hell may not want me to go back there
To let your healing waters flow over me
But I know now this is your call for me
And I will follow what your hand wants for me

I pray now for guidance
To deal with this spiritual warfare in my life
As my broken spirit begins its healing
So there will be no final barrier between us
And I come back to your water
So that I may live once again

255.
Walking forward in an empty plain
Nothing in sight but gravel and sand
The sun beating rays are burning
The skies cool grace abandoning
Faces of all the oppressors in life
Look down from the clouds above
Feel them spit curses at me
Feel their almighty arms as they hold me down

Dying inside

Walking through the forest late at night
Faces I can't see are brushing against me
Piercing branches are cutting me
Why are they all standing around me?
Don't they know when to leave us alone?
Why do they always attack me like this?
Now I can feel myself fuel this hate
Where is the escape, where is the grace?

Dying inside

And I slash my arms to bloody pieces
Siege my leg, slow my walk down
So many people never understand the pain
Feel it all day, everyday
Make the pain more intense to forget
About my heart, about my mind
Try to reach out to the hand to save me
But this knife of mine has captive me

Soul bleeding, body sieging
Thoughts unrelenting, I'm dying inside

256. God's Rose

Time has slowly ticked away
This year has been filled with shame
Brought on by myself
Since the first time I saw you
There was an angel watching over you
God already then had his arms surrounding you
It brings such joy now
To see that the rose has blossomed
God wanted you
Or you wouldn't be here now
Probably didn't know it at that time
What He would do through you
To bring me back to myself
To bring me back to Him

Shocked me right to the core
When you first came with our common friend
To commune in His presence
To let His spirit flow through you
Then one day your sin was lifted away
The rose was watered
So it could blossom
And shine in the night

Took a chance
Then I didn't know why
It's obvious now
To reach out and talk to you
In a far flung hope, we could be friends
Even though I had slipped into damnation
Tried to show you there was something more to me

I hated myself
It was so hard
Had to push so hard to get myself moving
To get myself to open up

Anyone that I had ever opened up to
Had only ever hurt me in my life
Didn't know whether you'd be another
For some God known reason I did
Even though I wanted to die
Even though I didn't care
God, I feel, pushed me
Guided my worthless hands
To at least say 'hi'

For He knew, I needed your friendship
For He knew that the night I cried in everyone's arms
For He knew, you'd say words that'd change my life
For He knew, I needed you to save me

The thornless rose
That made everything worth it
Encouraged me to continue on
Just by saying how much I've helped you
I still want to cry
Every time I think of it

You showed me
Just didn't tell me, but made me feel
That I'm not worthless or hopeless
I'm not damned
How can I ever thank you
Your God's rose
To a world that needed you

257. Catalyst

Mercy, confessions, testimonies all come at me
Don't know how to handle the flood
This influx of emotion thrown at me
It's overwhelming, and my heart screams
Screaming out the roar of life
I had been silenced once, long ago
But the need to be heard is coming back
All through the catalyst
Reactions start the healing process
Fire retakes my veins
The energy revives this undead corpse
I have refelt God's love
He chose a median to reach me I know
A way to react with and change me
To give me hope through words spoken yet read
One of His children, to touch me
To lead me back into this world
From a heavy world, a sorrowed world
Rejoice in the suffering of my old pain
Or it wouldn't have brought me to this place
'I can sing of His love forever'
Now that I can remember what it's about
Reshown to me, re-encouraged back into me
Through His child and my friend
I thank you God, for everything in my life
For my friends that you have shown your love through
Even this pain that has allowed me to reach my hand out
Bless them all, bless that one

258. My Prayer for You

This is my prayer for you
May you never see what I've seen
Or do things that I've done
To my world and to myself
Have His arms of love around you
So the hurt of sin may pass
Since I can't be with you now
I go all the distance I can to my knees
Don't deserve this kind of friendship
Done nothing in my life worth this
Yet I can feel your prayers around me
And it drives me to my knees
May you never hurt how I've hurt
Never feel alone in life again
Never have to say you're sorry
For regrets that will never leave
That you never cry to God to kill you
Or be afraid to see tomorrow
His angels I pray are with you
Protecting you from the world I know
From sins I've never said to you
And I pray to sweep your struggles away
That they may not burden you
To treasure life for you are precious
And shine to everyone around
This is my prayer for you
May you always be happy
May the joy you've been to me
Spread back to you
Keep that precious smile on your face
And feel His warm embrace
Since I can't be with you now
I fall to my knees

259. Play God

Dream of things I don't know why
See the faces all these thousand nights
It doesn't leave me but releases me
Till I wake up again screaming
Try to pass back off from reality
While I try to play God again

And I find myself here again
With the silver blade in my hand
This time digging for answers
Hidden deeper in the ignorant flesh
Truth screams out as I bleed
While I try to play God again

An angel before me reaches out
The words falling not too far off
Feel guilty for forcing myself away
Don't want to be seen like this
Can barely cope with myself
While I try to play God again

Pleading guilty in this lost cause
Forcing my hopelessness to the surface
Gagging on my heart as it comes up
All my hidden pain bubbles to the top
I try to hold myself together
While I want someone else to play God

I try to make myself look up
To put the light back in my sights
And heal the wounds, erase the scars
I can't live with this anymore
Replace the hate, replace this pain
Please play God in my life, be God in my life

260. Undead

Lost and confused, down to the ground
Fumbling through nothing
Needing to be extracted from my misery
Just barely touching the saving hands
Fell to death and away from life
Till someone came in for me
So grateful that each night I find myself crying
I'm alive again

I've touched the light, I'm undead
I live again, healed from myself
Reconstructed back to sanity
I see God's hand, reaching for me

Embraced the light yet I hide in night
So I can shine once again
Accepted back into the heaven's chorus
I had left under false beliefs
I'm alive again, I sing again
Never let myself fall again
Even now I find myself crying
Tears of resurrected joy

Undead, from old sorrows
Resurrected, from my hatred
You can never keep me down
So, blast your crimes at me

This new life has engulfed my soul
Full reversal of the monster
The killing beasts blood thirst drying
Need for vengeance receding
Handing out forgiveness
I can feel myself flying
You can never keep me down
Cuz one day I'll fly with Him in the clouds

Even though you can kill my flesh
My soul is immortal again
When the final trumpet sounds
You'll see me rise again

261.
I see your face, and I cry
Your smiling grace, I cry
So close yet so far, I cry

I think of the joy brought to me
Is this how my feelings should be
Although I smile, it's hard
To see how I really feel

Cuz I don't want to accept this
Don't want to feel this way

Damnation surrounds me
Yet I see past the veil
To your eyes
These tears I draw, or is it joy instead?
Is my happiness leaking from me?
Should I laugh or sob
Mourn or praise

The darkness I bear
Is it starting to pass through me?

Remember the sound of the angel's wings
Flapping as I was raised
Wings you carry with you
When I remember your grace
Am I understanding too much?
That I can't see the real?
When I see you as a new creation
Not as what you were before
Are these tears for real?
Is what Jehovah put in my heart real?
Or am I just hallucinating again
Said you were gonna call me
How much I want to hear your voice

A hug for my mind
Just like your sweet embrace
How I wish you were here
Sitting beside me
For a shoulder to lean to and cry on

Why do I feel this way?
Thinking of you
I have to wipe the tears away

262.
All I know right now
Is that I want to be more than this
When in your arms I feel I can escape
Where demons have no grasp on my soul
Is this true to me or have I lost control
Is heaven so far away from me?
Get lost in the hazeful mist
As it overtakes my mind
Conscious running away while I lay there compromised
My hopes all lie in tomorrow
Why is it always today?
Is heaven so far away for me
As I cry out to God, I wonder
When will He answer me?
There are days I feel I could fly
And yet others I just want to die
Will this sad circle ever end?
Is heaven so far away from me?
Plead for God to save me
As I see you standing there, in my mind
Scream and find myself bleeding
While the moon reflects away from me
Father save me, Father please
Or is heaven so far away from me

263.
I am waiting
Waiting for you to come home
Waiting for your arms around me
I am waiting, I am waiting

264. Bloodroses

I
Are you still inside feeding?
Faces that are always haunting
Depression striking deeper
Corrupts me to angry fits of malice
Lies that I fed to myself
Are my only truth teachers
No tongues to ever speak of hope
Mind full of nothing worth remembering
Tears ever screaming
Watering my facial skin
Drawn from reserved pools
That I'd rather shed on a shoulder
While blasphemizing my heart
Hide the pain for another day
Smiling through concrete frowns
Darkness just can't be hidden
Siege's the only proof of life
In bitter bloody agony
Red clouds the vision
Of angels I can't see
Filters through my enemies
Image reflecting back at me
Time a relentless acid
The road crumbling before me
Bridge across the fiery chasm
Already fallen, broken, hurting
Life just not worth the living
My family has left me bleeding
I'm so alone
No reason to try
No reason to stop crying

II
Rejected fields of broken love

Trying to forget the need
Yet feeding it my heart
Comfort receding from the thorn
Opening to everything yet nothing
Silenced by artificiality
Genuine feelings fabricated
Attitudes masqueraded as light
Following a path of unsmoothed stone
Wanting not needing
Selfishness setting the sun
I fall crying, trying
To stumble out of this rut
False angels singing to me
Of friendships bound by walls
Outside marooned by emotional wreckage
Rescued me to kill
Death so overwhelming
Yet allow myself to be resurrected
Wings of broken promises
Sprout to bring me down
Pain unparalleled by anger
But yet nothing is so sure
Joy unrejoiced by happiness
All I want is to hear
Sound ever escaping
Noise never resonating
Heart stolen from this pedestal
While I try to forget everything
Running from nothing
Because it's all in my own fantasies

III

Sweet nectar of a tasteless blight
Mask of hate with pretty eyes
Boiling vengeance roaming unscathed
Scaring blade and forceful tears
Emotional detachment satisfying
Tears of no one's cares

Petals falling to the asphalt
Lunatics foaming their screams
Drops of blood unfermenting
Soothing bottle ever raping
Forceful prayers to silent eyes
Green dreams to unreasonable
Wasted tears to angry fears
Angels watching while I'm laughing
You blasphemize my salvation
Deny myself unknown necessities
Lay here waiting
Nighttime that's forever young
Broiling hatred for myself
Exposing all you lies
Can't believe, can't receive
On my knees while I bleed
Faltered and so distracting
Though this was so right
Again I'm wrong
Alienation of everyone for nothing
Self-presentation takes its hold
Drive away to another day
Keep feeding lies
Soul face so evident
Take this away from me

265.
You are ...
The pedal on the dried rose
A star in the moonless night
The trickle of a dried creek
A leaf at winter's door
The music in an empty theatre
A song that hasn't been written
The door to a dying heart
A cry from a newborn child
The black in the fresh snow
A tree in the forsaken desert
The green grass after drought
A bloody war that saves
You are ...

266.
Every time I look into your eyes
I want to run away, escape this heart
I've been enslaved by my emotion
The chains are weighing me down
Invisible enemies ever taunting me
Trying to drag me away from His place
I stay, unwanting, force myself to stand
And not run away from your eyes
Demons rip at my insides relentlessly
Trying to make me bleed my soul to them
This war that is waged forever within me
Gets more and more vicious each passing day
As each side contends for my frailty
And though the night seems long the sun will rise again
Temptress, I push myself away for both our good
Yet Almighty God won't let me go
As much as it hurts, He wants me to endure it
For what? I don't understand, not yet

267.
Take away my dignity
Strike at me
Leave nothing to fall back on
Spine is gone
Have no will of my own
Go back to this place
Where I left myself standing
Just barely hanging on
By less than a thread
All faith is gone
No faith is left
I can't do this
Why should I
Let out my rage
Let out my hate
Sick of the way
The way you make me feel
Now you give me a power
Power to play God
That's not my right
Don't put this burden on me
Lift this from me
You worry about me
Then put this stress on me
Why don't you be the one who cuts me?
Your words the knife that makes me bleed
When I look in your eyes
Your innocence is evident to me
I could never tell you
So, forget you, forget this, forget everything

268.
I see your face I can't escape you
As fast as I run, you're always there
Tried to face off this touch inside me
Burned the light ever since I first saw you
Yet it burns brighter the more I try
The more I try to make it go away
Now as the new sun breaks a new dawn
I pray it'll burn me unlike yesterdays

269.

Never saw anything
Yet found myself watching
Not knowing what to search for
Everything was clouded
Nothing was real
The voice ever haunting
Pulling ever at my soul
Finally convincing
Body constantly being sieged
Never knew you
Couldn't give a thought about anyone
Didn't want to see you
Standing there mocking me
Now as I stand here
See the failure I've become
See the failures I've endured
Stop feeding me lies
Just tell me the truth
Or is there no light in your life
I've got my own darkness
I don't need yours either
Get out of me
Get out of my life
Separate me
Split apart my emotions
There's nothing left for me
Let me burn
Let me burn

270.

Try to love nothing, yet I cry for everything
Close my eyes for something, to let it be meaningless
Stab myself to kill my heart, bleed out the emotion
As my spirit fights this war against my mind
No one sees the pain I fight each day in life
Hold out my hand its shot away, left to lick my wounds again
Just let it bleed and let angels carry me off
To see my maker so he can judge me and let me die
Can never hope for salvation in this life
Take away tomorrow to escape the next tear
Please God, I love you, come and save me
I have nothing left here to live for
Why make me continue to live through this hatred
Lift from me the suffering of the new dawn

271.

Broken I stand
Running, running away
This doesn't make any sense
Unrelentless attacks
Strengthening my feeble soul
Yet I just want to fly away
God grant me peace
To escape myself
So blind I cannot see
I try to kill everything
Try to tell me everything's ok
It will all work out someday
They don't now anything about me
And how I've failed
God reveal yourself to me
Just give it up and let me sleep now
Deep inside I know
Something isn't right
Get on my feet
To take another hit
Why do I have to give?
Dying inside again
Laughing as I bleed
Is everything ok in me?

272.

Nothing matters when you cry
All the pain you've held inside
With all the crimes you try to hide
Now they're all exposed to everything
Shed your tears water this hate
Despise the creatures you create
Your heart has just died again
Envision yourself though others eyes
While your imagined lies pass by and by

273.

Singing starts, I can barely hear them
As my heart is weighed on once again
Drop to my knees sacrificing my dignity
Praises wrap around my conscience
The worship helps to lift my hearts cry
Whisper under my breath my worries
Of how I love yet fear and feel unworthy
Not knowing where my worries are tonight
Pray to God to relieve my sorrow
But it stays to I pray and cry more
Angels keep singing around me
Of hope, praise and how happy I should be
But it won't happen until I know
That these tears on my face aren't for nothing
Making me want to say all these prayers
So everything will be ok
I thank God for this friendship in my life
That makes me want to live on
Feel like this dark world can't touch me
For I for once, mean something to someone
And all I want is to see their face
Even if it's from afar, where they can't see too
So my heart can rest again
Knowing everything at least seems ok
See their smiling face again
This demonhood has passed from me
The dark child is falling away

274.
Never asked for anything
Left the minds wondering empty
To not find anything that could make me stumble
Make me bleed
Asked for no gift from heaven
Just leave me surrounded in these lies
I created about myself
Stop paining me
Every chance you get
Let me deny myself of everything
So I can't fell it
So I won't get consumed
Yet it still grows in me
It feels so cold
The pain of taking
What was never mine
Don't want what you offer me
If when I humbly ask for nothing
I receive the worlds hate
I've never wanted anything
Just let me die

275.
Help
Can someone hear my cry
Is anyone out there
They all left
Except those voices
That resound forever within me
Watch myself in the mirror
As the beast takes hold
Watch myself die through his eyes
Unable to regain control

- No one cares
- They see my tears
- But they shrug me off
- No one cares
- They see my wounds
- But they mock my pain

Draw my sleeve
Feel the blood rush through
Waiting to be released
He grabs a handle
I see the lightning flash across the blade
Feel the pain he's causing me
Someone stop him please
No one hears my cries
The blood slips down my arm
Warm river bathes my flesh
Beg for mercy
As I see myself going home

- I don't want to go home
- Not yet
- I've got too much to live for
- I've got too much to cry for
- They don't feel my pain

\- They don't see my tears
\- No one cares
\- Until you're dying
\- They knew all this time
\- But they did nothing
\- Now I've let my sanity slip
\- The pressure too much for me
\- No one cares about me
\- Why should I care about myself?
\- Obviously not worth it
\- Don't spend your time worrying about me
\- Never have before, why start now
\- Just get away from me
\- And let me die

Someone stop him
My flesh can't bear much more

-Look at what the world has done to me
-Look what they've driven me too
-I wanna die
-Let me die
-Let me bless the world
-Casting out this misblessing
-Let
-Me
-Die

Dear God
What am I doing?
What have I done?
So much hate driven in me
That I now hate myself
Give me back control
Give me back myself

\- Said you loved me
\- Why have you hurt me?

\- Yahweh Yir'eh, my provider
\- Provider of nothing
\- Except this black widow
\- I've used to destroy
\- It's relieving
\- Looking forward to going beyond
\- Where the pain is nothing
\- Where this fool will get what he deserves
\- So naive
\- He knew nothing

Want nothing more
Than to be hugged one last time
But no one cares
No one's here

276.

Unknown landscape
Viewed from corrupted eyes
Oppressed from every angle
Night sounds sirens unstopping
So much blood, pure, innocent
Escaped here to new bondage
Yet the chains are looser
With more eyes watching
Silver mirrors offer no more joy
Harassing demons are gone
The only voice in this desert
In my head is my own
Angels stand guard over this
Safer than ever before
Yet so far away
Desires of my mind still haunting
When all I want is to see those eyes
Painful reminder kept hidden
Try to talk aloud
Yet kept in silence
By fears of this new place
So many obstacles
Placed intentionally in the mind
Will be forced to overcome
God help me
I can't do this alone

277.

Silence overcomes me
The music slowly fades
Yet the transformation continues
Soul softly hums praises to the king
Can't remember my worries
Heart beats out a song
To which my soul softly sings
His spirit transforms it into a worthy thing
Feel the pain sitting out
Through hardships and fears
Everything seems to fade
I gaze to the throne
'Cause you've changed me within
Everything seems to fade out
Hang my hurts on a cross
Which you've taken for me
All the pains run away
It can't take this joy
I now have in my heart

278.

Here we go again
This time it's different
You're in my land
In my dominion
The upper hand is mine
You'll hafta fight harder
To draw my blood
In order to water the blood thirsty soul
Strength I sought has been found
I was nothing now I'm everything
I'll be breathing down your neck
This time the pistol is mine
You are nothing
Take your best shots
Cuz that's all you get
It won't be enough
Reincarnation of new flesh
I will take you on
Fight me with fire
I'll use a supernova
Hope you like it in hell
I'm gonna send you there
Forever bound
Welcome to the new war

279.
Take me home now
I can't take anymore
I see the roads end
Feel so pitiful
So insecure, doubting myself, I can't feel
Hopes for today and slowly draining away
Don't know what I'm doing
I feel that I'm drowning
Tears are choking
In this humble abyss I'm falling
Show me my fears, show me the hate
Put me back in my place
Here I am in the city of angels
I had told you, I showed you

280.
Drowning, I black out
All the pain that is evident in me
The people I trust are so far away
I can't feel their loving embrace
Spoken words move my heart
As I cry myself away
My friend I love
Though you're so far away
I feel your heart here with me
Spend another night mourning, weeping
For a touch lost in the folds of travel
Though God is with me I feel so alone
There brothers can't fill that void
I wish for nothing more
Than to come home
And see something go right in my life
Feel like I've lost a diamond inside
The diamond is what I need today
Want to feel the only embrace
That I wanted in my life
The world seemed so small there
Now it's gone, now it's gone
All I desire is to see you again
These pictures don't do anything
I have to hide them away
Or I'll constantly be missing you
More than my heart already does
Can't see through these tears anymore
Everything is falling away
I'm falling away

281.
Live forever in this torment
Shine light so blinding
Take out the needing
Or this particular feeble flesh
Kill all the wanting
Cuz it's all so trivial
Make out with death
Dates that promise results
Make visible the lies
Wrapped in misunderstanding
Bind the demons
That force my hands to slaughter
Ungrateful dreams
That chew away thought process
Screw all the pretenses
That feed stupid assumptions
Reveal the evil
That's destroying me
I am victorious
No one can kill me
I cannot be taken down
Darkness reign over me
Jesus
Rescue me, salvation
I am free

282.
I feel there is nothing more to me
To fill me and comfort me
Shrieks of joy so encouraging
While I hope for more, blissful peace

Tear drops fall nowhere
Forced tear spouts to dry out
Try to surface the sadness in my heart
My mourning has come
Deaths spirits harassing
This feeble broken soul
Rivers of remorse course through me
Try to wonder why

This heart feels so empty
A void come alive within
When I had to leave
All reality left behind
Back to the beginning of the spiral
That has no foreseeable end
Misery entraps me in conscious
Losing touch forever

Save me I cry from this
Hearing you was good enough for me
As I was forced to retire
My heart screamed out its ache
As I try to convince myself not of this
Or the distance I've come away from you
Feel like seeing myself once more
But for what? you'd still be gone

Longing for nothing more
Then when the winters grace falls upon us
God sends his gift to earth
Likewise I'll see you again

I'll survive the raging hell storms
Though death may try to claim me
The hurt may swell within
But I will come home

Nighttime brings such peace
As I pass away from this
It hurts but I'm strong enough
To wait till I see you again
Force myself through this day
Each one brings unrivaled pain
I'm sure I'll be crying again
When dusk emerges the sun

So many words spoken to me
So many faces try to bring peace
In my solemn heart I know
There's only one peace to come
It drives me on to go all the way
Keep hoping for the future
Though I wish that that would release me
But I'll wait, I'll wait

283.

Look at the pictures
I'm falling forever
My heart is aching
Not soothing, never breaking
Straining constantly, the pressure is building
Forcing the trauma
Just living is scarring
The senses are deadening
This body's preparing
For inevitable release
Edges sharpening
Edges dropping
The chasm deepening
Sounds swallowing
Mouth unopening
Is this the only road
That this pain leads down?
Tragic ends not fazing
Tears, not caring
These faces I want
Don't want to be here
Want to go home
Cuz there is peace
Let my heart sink
In this emotional pit
Where's the peace
All I feel is pain

284.

At the brink of new destruction
Contemplating my wants, desires
Forcing out things I don't wanna see
But that I face each day
Bring out the knife to escape
To open the vents frustrating
Gaze at old scars I bear
Feel them calling to me

Is there something more?
Something else to be?

Jesus, my Lord
Rescue me form all this
Your angels are singing
Let me hear them
Sit here drowning
Misery getting the best of me
Take this away from me
These subtle wants
Screaming desires
I just can't take this anymore
Give me release
I need you

Here I go now
To the abyss
Can't turn back now
Save me

285.
Where have you gone?
Been taken away from me
Put you on a pedestal
So I would never forget
Now feeling I've lost
This battle is my heart
My soul screams for mercy
This flesh hurts more everyday
The rose is gone
I've lost touch with myself
Force down so much pain
Make myself forget
The cure forever lost
Hope is flying away

286.
Break
You can't take this
Everything on you
Pressurizes your thoughts
Wrap your conscious in silicon
Take you out for a round

Nothing makes sense anymore
How could I explain it to you?
This damage is catastrophic
My control is slipping away
Run away before I hurt you
All your help could fall in vain

Don't push me
The monster is sleeping inside
It knows what to do to me
Humbling it destroys me
Don't let these scars pass to you
Everything will be taken away

This friendship unequalled
God's never given me someone like you
All this pain seems so contagious
I don't want to infect you too
Leave now before I crumble
Strip you down to strained foundations

I'll see you sometime on the outside
Where people never stop singing His name
I'll be there waiting for you
At the pearl gates of heaven
Where happiness is forevermore
Where this pain does not exist

287.
Silence presses on me
Stare into all your eyes
Think you know everything
Everything is feeble lies
Fabricate your minds
To what you think I should be
Don't try to mold me
It'll only drive you insane
When I break your casts
All illusions will fall away
I am nothing
Of what you thought I should be
Why don't you open your minds?
Let my expression be free
Too busy sorting everything in my life
To play your roles, to play your games

288.
Angel, shining one
Where is this heart of mine?
Lost my unwanted emotions
In the midst of chaotic pain
Bring me new salvation
In this hour, my desire
Lost in the blade of my hate
Fighting for survival
Want to see the light
Stay alive till it comes to save me
The way I feel, is not natural
No smile on my face
Yet everything that haunts me
Flees away to the brink
When you're here with me
Never let me go
I can't stand alone
My knees are weakened
Shoulders can't carry the burden
Please help me
Take me home

289.
My faith is alive
The dead will arise
River runs through me
My tears are ripped away
The pain crumbles
My walls fall down
In emotion I triumph
Stronger than ever
Flower reblooms
This new light has come

290.
Ran to this place but it wasn't enough
The pain has followed, the pain has come
Sing His praises inside of my head
While His arms embrace me
No children here in my life
Jesus Christ is with me inside
The dagger tip still drills in my mind
Is there solace for this chaotic time?

291.
Everything's distorted now
Can't make sense anymore
Out of all this
Tests I've written before
Haven't I passed before
Why should I do this again?
Dear God, what is your purpose in this
Can't see past the vein, blood pulsing
Vengeance is eating at me, I want to
Bleed myself away, like yesterday
Clotheslined on my knees
Slain by spiritual grief
Rap my head on the floor
Knock my head on the floor
Can't see straight anymore
Rage has clouded over my sight
Love isn't reaching to me
God make me feel your love

292.
Don't need you
Why did I even try?
To think you'd accept me
But you wouldn't I knew it
But I tried anyways
All this effort not worth it
Why should I try anymore?
Wanted to be more
Everyone's bent on still holding me down

293.

Your face is hidden
But I can still see your pain
Empty eyes misleading
Hollow touch seduces me
I sold you a piece of my heart
No receipt to prove it
Fed of my blood
While I ran away hiding
Try to take away from me
Everything you think I am
But you can never take away
What I have inside me
Cuz you gave it to me
It has become all that I am
You can't take my soul away
So, stop trying my unwanted tormentor
See you all the time
I don't know why
Voice resounds inside my head
It reeks of ignorance
No trace of anything
Just empty space
Where something that once was me
Lived in humble peace
Now I'm fighting against myself
Your demonic memories
You'll never take my life away from me
For you are nothing, I am something
Are you ready for me?
Then lock and load

294.
Sit here
Unknowing
Pain-scape unequalled
Where's the sorrow
The sympathy
Forget this
This isn't worth it
What the hell am I living for?
To wake up each day hurting
The drugs they gave me don't solve anything
This pain I feel is killing me
Killing me
Nothing left in my mind
Mechanical releases consuming
Unrelenting fervor
I can't imagine
What it's like to be you
With the smile on your face
What is in you, I don't have
My own hand is killing me
I wanna die
Forget it
I can't think straight
Everything is ending
In my mind, overdrive
Why should I be the last one standing?
Just to be alone again
I don't want this
I wanna die
I wanna die

295.
Dear God come to me
I need you, I'm hurting
The legions assaulting
Voices I can't escape
Their crushing my mind
Controlling my life
Want to stay in control
My soul forever be mine
Can't take it away
Can't force me away

296.

I see a great city in the clouds
No walls, no boundaries
Never darkness, always light
The sunlight shines forever
Silver and gold banners shimmer in the wind
The sword no longer falls
The leader has been defeated
Only voices heard are not my own
But praises to the king, never ceasing
Angel's smile as we walk the streets
For we have finally come home
The wars we have fought are over
No longer do our souls cry for peace
The blade no longer falls upon me
Pain has become unfamiliar, uncomforting
The need for mourning has passed
No longer do tears fall at all
Sorrow that has been part of us has left
Death does not haunt us
For finally we have overcome it
And passed through it
Joy is part of us now
Happiness has overcome our suffering
Everyone we've lost is there
No one is denied this joy
Victory is finally ours
Forever and ever
We will praise the king forever
For salvation has come

A Shadow's Cry: The Fires of Judgment

Chapter 1: The Illusion

1.

Ancient stones and temples old
Where ancient secret lie
Lie mysteries we cannot know
Of times that lived and died.
What ancient race lived on these grounds?
In the jungle that surrounds?
We're they barbaric or else civilized?
Which stories did they tell?
Ancient winds blow the tales
To ears that cannot hear
Of monsters and giants grand
That lived and fought for only time knows.
Ancient king's carbon empty thrones
Of cold yet mobile stone
The harem halls stand to say
Of the desires of powerful hearts.
Artifacts so old they're dust
Speak of sophistication of old
Yet minds can't understand how primitive man
Could read the stars and sky.
Their tales are told in forgotten woods
That can't be understood
But one day the many warn loud
What their downfall was.

Can modern man learn these tales
To not repeat mistakes
The future yet is untold to all
They can only wait and see.

2.
Rain pours down
Soothing anxious hearts
Bringing calm to the raging wind
Smell of dew fills your breath
With the joy of
Life.
Soft pitter-patter renews the mind
The soul settles its nerves
The brokenness mended
In the crushed grass
From children playing
Now jumping in puddles
Screams of delight.
Thunder booms its mighty voice
That all may herd the call
To listen to the rain
As it falls
Ever downward.
Making us see
Life
At ultimate work
Ever flowing circles
Of streams in the gullies.
Cheerful trickles
Down the windows
As we bask in the warmth
To listen.

3. Birth of a Star

A great expanse of mist and gas
Where fires wait to start
The mysteries that await here
Are not so understood.
What incident could begin the flame?
To begin a star anew
That may give life or wait patiently
For discovery in people's eyes.
Twisting vortices try to force the spark
But silently it doesn't give
Gravity continues to draw all in
The cloud to a standing state.
But fire starts, to bring new life
To the newly born space bound light
What tale will it one day tell
Is for anyone to guess,

4. Dark Wood

Rustling trees of oak and pine
Line many winding trails
Leaves and needles both give claim
To the hidden secrets within.
Where creatures come out to eat and play
In their long natural home
While the sun is high in sky
The creatures make their nests.
Children come out to explore its groves
Hoping for something new
Destructive hands snap and pull
At the foliage of olden days.
Laughter fills the hollow wood
As young ones play their games
The creatures hide in fear of them
Not knowing what to do.
When darkness falls, nocturnal ones
Come out to guard the night
Their watchful eyes keep out all
Who would do the dark wood harm.
The chirps and moans give easy fright
To all who come too near
But they too are more afraid
Of what is given credit for.
But light will come back with the day
To silence the nightly watch
The creatures come out to play once more
In the quietly rustling trees.

5. Jewels of Night

Across the majestic, glorious expanse
Comes much but little light
Tiny diamonds in the darkened sky
Offer hope to navigators and dreams to children.
A drape of black with tiny pinholes
Sprinkling out such precious life
Mysteries we held in wonder
As watchers learn all that may be.

Light may have expired but still is seen.

Dreams are made in twinkling lights
That cover time and space
While these small jewels hold their place
Over generations who dream.

6. Luna

Silver maiden
Hanging in the night sky
Pulling at the ocean tide.
Worshipped by ancient ones
With little return for such faith.
Pulling at strings of madness
Losing minds in the turmoil.
Though set so far from Gaia's touch
The distance has been traversed.
Will we walk once more across her face?
Or leave her to sleep?
Nay,
She awaits.
The new frontier we have yet to best
In gripping wonder.
To see as she sees
And wonder as she wonders.

7. Symphony

The evening comes
The chords are strung
The symphony starts to play

Hushing sounds
Along concert grounds
Introduce the musical cascade

People listen
While music strings glisten
Out marvelous inviting sound

The majestic road
And emotions soar
As hearts are overtaken

When tears do fall
For joy of all
The bands so touching songs

Never was heard
A glorious merge
Of brass and strings alike

Yet the music faces
Like the end of a day
The roar of clapping begins

8. The Tower

Alone and abandoned on an ancient isle,
With no inhabitants in its stone marble walls,
The Tower stands, noble and proud.
What race of ancient ones held its secrets?
Were mysteries of old, sought in its bowels?
Or weapons of war constructed in the courtyard?
The winds whisper through the surrounding forest,
Whispering the ancient tales in the breeze,
Yet no creature is around to hear them.

The nearby sea laps its tide against the white walls,
Washing away all weary stains of time,
Cleansing the very soul of forgotten darkness.
Will light once more illuminate the halls?
What children ever played games in the grass?
Did a king ever rule from the empty throne?
The empty library holds no more wondering scholars,
Stars shine on the long cleared out battlements,
Only El-Shaddai knows who will next call the tower home.

9. Tree-King

In a hidden glade, in darkened woods
A mighty king holds court
Where pixies and sprites do their dances
In his mighty over-reaching arms.
Leaves that grow a crown on his head
And bark, his royal court
He holds his court for all the creatures
That come to enjoy his comfort.
Little fairies dance and sing
To ease his rising mood
At man who would dare to encroach his court
And hold all under his sway.
Satyrs hold court as guards
To hold back the coming darkness
As he makes ready to make fools of men
And reveal mysterious faults.
Faults they know but refuse to believe
But will force them to see
Till once again they flee in fright
At the Tree-King's majesty.
Then all the creatures will sing his songs
As he barks in the life giving sun
And lets his kingdom rest again
Till the creatures once again call his name.

Chapter 2: The Reality

10.

Tell me O Lord, why the wicked prosper,
Their ways seem so easy and carefree,
The struggles of life are not as stressed,
By the task obliging in righteousness.

Yet they curse and mock your name,
I cannot stand to hear their mocking,
Their thoughts are not consumed with you,
And I cannot separate my thoughts.

Lash out in anger, O God,
Do not stand for their evil forever,
Let them know the wrath in your arm,
Unleash the arsenal of heaven.

Their ways are empty and meaningless,
They can never find true fulfillment,
Longing for answers the scholars cannot give,
Yet they feel they can mock your assurances.

Fill me with your presence, O Lord,
Keep my heart firm in your gentle hands,
Let your breath warm my spirit,
May your thanks be ever on my lips.

11.
Looking into the jaws of death
This pit of iniquity and sin
Feeling my soul slowly pulled out
To be laid on an altar of sin
Try to justify staying
But holiness keeps telling me to leave
Yet the chains of hell have bound me so
Cannot escape, can not be free

12.
Lord my flesh is weak
My mind is filled with corruption
When I smell this world's perfume
I crumble into acts of sin.
Remember me my God,
Help me to rise above such iniquity
Keep my thoughts pure and holy
So that I may honor you.

13.
The night's minds eye reveals to all
Desires of every whim
Twisted dreams and soothing tides
Of delirium and fantasy.
Sometimes scenes of frightening sights
Harass at every turn
Checking over the shoulder
Or crying in turmoil.
A dark hall engulfing
Steady hands knocking
Causing a pause
To scream or die.
Killers await in the silent room
Where solace is nightly found
Demonic thoughts plague all hope
As all wait for never coming dawn.

14.
All I feel is the pain you put in me
A blazing coal eating away
The fire consumes my kindled soul
Leaving nothing but hate for all you've done to me.
Try to pass the day away at the bottom of a bottle
All that's left inside has been burned away
A calloused heart that feels nothing but pain
And rage for what you've brought to me.
A simple no would have avoided so much of this
Instead, the leash got tighter and stronger
Making me crave the solitude of death
To get you to finally go away.
But that's a dream that will never pass to truth
Everyday your face is haunting me
The thickening blood doesn't wash it all away
Just causes me to drown and never find release.

15.
Where is justice?
Where is equality?
When evil men rise up in triumph
Showing all the world their accomplishments
Do the unrighteous deserve this more?
What dark pacts have they made?
There seems to be no end to misery
As righteousness the rock on which I stand
There is joy that comes
In the small and quiet voice
May it be a guide out of this despair
And thrust me into ever welcoming light.

16.

Darkness dripping in the void
Silencing startled cries
Absorbing desperate shouts
To enter at its own glee.
Patient and ponderous it moves along
Not caring how long it takes
To enshroud the heart of mortal man
And claim him as its own.
Fighting is futile as it cannot be shunned
For its in the very heart
Of everyone both pure and not
Their secret little truth.
Slowly it feeds the black dogs wrath
To overcome the white dogs justice
It waits, immortal, inconceivable
To take over every man.

17.

Are privileged lives an excuse to kill?
Unsavory lawyers saying wealth makes us sick
Not having to take full responsibility
For the unnecessary deaths at their hands.
There is no justice left
When rich men think they are gods
And judges bow to their egos
Judgement is due from on high.
For such lack for a consideration of life
Yahweh looks down ashamed
Not wanting to show His face on such injustice
Yet we keep silent.
Not wanting to risk having our petals plucked
If we don't speak out then the rich will continue
Self-entitlement and false gods will reign.
Justice has become a joke
When the killers are set free
Little limitations unimpeding
Mothers still coddling their sons.
Wake up world!
Shall we continue the charade?
Justice must be done.
As the blood cries out from the ground
Yahweh calls out to the corrupt
To stand up for what is right
Not for the appeal of gold.

18.
Giving in to base desires
Like mangeful dogs, bitten and devoured
Donkeys slowly plodding along
Pulling a cart of their own sin.
Yet you say we are enlightened!
That you have risen above base desires!
Hypocrite! You give in to your instincts daily
Rejecting Yahweh's law on your heart.
Feed your sin like a ravishing hound
Consuming your pitiful soul
Do not say you are better
When you reject the one who gave you breath.
Call on His name
The Holy One of Israel
Feel the power of His love
Be restored by His salvation.
Then you will once more stand
Stand as the image of the coming Yahweh
Know freedom and faith
And be truly made whole.

19.
Company of fools
Ignorant to the truth of Yahweh
Believing themselves to be gods
Noses held high
Dogs smelling their own filth
As they revel in destructive accomplishments
A broken tankard
With no tears to spill
For a deserted temple of the Spirit
Forsaken barren wasteland
With no true life
Yet fools drink to their destruction
Open sealed eyes
See the death of all salvation
That Yahweh strives to save
Behold the folly
Of believing you are the one
Before being cast down to Gehenna.

20.

All they see is darkness.
Yet we tell them our secrets
Rely on the void to bring us home
Not trusting in light to show us truth
Rather believing the lie.
All they see is darkness.
Thinking we have some special truth
We deny Yahweh His due
Thinking Heaven is falsehood and lies
Not accepting truth though it follows.
All they see is darkness.
Why do we trust in broken dreams?
Lies told us to become intimate friends
Put faith in objects we revere like gods
Or modern warriors we sell ourselves to.
All they see is darkness.
Can we turn and believe in the true Word?
Discover the reason we were born?
Do we believe enough to be saved?
Can we bear it all like Calvary's cross?
All they see is darkness.
Rather count on the world and be dismayed
Do our drugs and drink our wines
Refusing to turn and be healed
Be seeing but blind, hearing but deaf.
All they see is darkness.

21.

Might of humanity in steel light
On an island consumed by greed
A fortress of the world
The new Babylon, Shinar.
Where the kings of our world
Boast of their greatness
Many nations cry to them for aid
Yet they demand terms for service.
The national gods dictate the rules
Break them when they see fit
The whore called Babylon
Risen once more.
Shall unrighteousness rule our world?
Will black gold determine our fares?
As Chaldean kings say what is next
O World, cry for deliverance!
Let the blood of martyrs speak!
Have we fallen so far from grace?
Call on Yahweh!
Shun the Babylonian whore!
Taken flesh in nations united
Believing they are gods
But they too will kneel before the lawless one.
And be judged by Christ's fire
For defining the earth
For fornication with the dragon.

22.
Try to bleed away all of the pain
As my sin brims up over the day
Searing light reminds me of the cries
I screamed out in the midst of my strife.

Can't bleed anymore, there's nothing left to hide
Touch the burning coal, to wipe away the night
Reach to the light, find grace for the strain
Scars I hide, brought out from my fright.

Dear God, you have shown yourself to me
Though I still hide, there's nowhere I can flee
My broken soul cries out to your love
To make me whole and give you my all.

Yet I will cut with the pain
Try to bleed it away
When I can't breathe
You lift me on high

Take away the hurt, I am whole, I am right
These fears I hold won't conquer me
The gracious grace that I've tried to deny
Is undeniable and makes me good inside.

23.

I'll wear a mask, so you can't see inside
And all the pain that holds to me
The fears that keep me up at night
Carry over in the light as a waking dream.
Lord, save me, as I die inside
I want to hold on to your hand
That guides me through this waking hell
Where people try to take me down.
I've hated, I've loved, I've carried it all
Fulfillment I have they try to rip away
Hold on to this cross as I bleed out pain
For trying to be a bigger person this way.
Though I'm shackled to pain, I know I'm free
While I hide the scars that aren't shown
Ridiculed and criticized, for standing in the right
As I try to show freedom and not hurt inside.

24.

Crying out from broiling hate
The world cannot understand
Its eyes are shut to the truth
Blinded by its own misdeeds.
Hungry suffer choosing vices over need
While the wealthy horde their stores
No one thinks there's need for a saviour
Yet wrong, so wrong.
Everyone believes they will live on
Yet Nihilism must take hold
No one can accept inevitability of death
Ever pushing onward.
Accept your saviour, stop the lies
Corrupting Solomon's legacy of wisdom
Using our brains to the point of detachment
While we suffer in inner silence.
Reach out to the light
Renew us, for the love we behold
The only one that can carry our burdens
Yet we resist being made whole.
Wicked world accepts the truth
Gods love is what you need
To reach out and help the hurting
And pass the burden back to the thoughtless one.

25.
Yahweh Almighty
Closed minds can't fathom you
Hurting hearts don't long for you
Too many people believe in themselves
Rather than on their makers hand.
You raise nations before you
You tear them down in a nightfall
All in one act of judgement
Does your holiness make itself manifest.
If only the hurting could see you
They would turn and be healed
But their pride goes before their fall
Just as their master of light did.
Turn all our hearts, oh God
Heal us all of Sun's affliction
Before the fires of judgement come
As we stand her unaware.

26.
Flaunting riches
In the face of the lowly
Arrogance to accompany
We don't live as you do
In your perfect little world.
Get scolded
For having an opinion
May Yahweh humble you
For thinking you're better
Not thinking about those under you.
Why should we suffer?
The dark side of your pride?
Why should we bleed?
From cuts you inflict?
Judgement is coming
Too proud to see the signs
The fires will burn around you
Yet pride and unrepentance
Will consume you.

27.
Time,
Does something so linear
Have to proceed in a straight line?
Can the swirling eddies of eternity
Adjust the process of inevitability?
Like joyful swirls of children playing?
Or dangerous loops of leaves in the winds?
Even eternity, ever moving forward
Just an eternal, everlasting creator
Existing, ruling
Time a creation of Yahweh's hand
Making it impossible for Him to be subject to it.
Can a king be commanded by His peasant?
Or a sun be acted on by a moon?
To say it so of God, Heresy!!!
So, the eternal God to time,
Neither subject to it nor bound by it
Ever able to change its course
To stop the sun in the days of Joshua, a swirl?
Or reversing the shadow to king Hezekiah, a loop?
Truth is we may never know
Time an enigma of Yahweh
To make us patient
While we wait for Him
To make us yearn
As we worship Him
When the eschaton comes, and we see His glory
Forevermore, Amen.

28.
Depravity
People dancing around on stages
Being something they're not
Slapping Yahweh in the face
For Entertainments sake.

Depravity
People lusting after carnal relations
Sicknesses forcing unnatural unions
Claiming Yahweh is wrong
For Gratifications sake.

Depravity
Bowing a knee to false gods
Praising them as they perform on stage
Denying that Yahweh is God
All for Fulfillments sake.

Will the world not listen?
Will people not see?
Turn, be healed
But, no
Sin has taken hold
All that is left
What this world has become
Depravity

29.
Flirt with the thought of death
Of blood twinkling down your arm
Life slowly slipping away
As you drop the blade on the floor.
Is this what Yahweh really wanted?
When the saints weren't allowed to do so?
When the refuge cities were set up,
To save them from a reaper's grip?
Self-inflicted death,
A thought from foreign gods.
How can Yahweh heal you!
How can He use your pain,
To save someone else that is lost?
Can you be redeemed after death?
Pain isn't worth it.
Will the devil's laughter
Echo through your soul
After you leave your flesh
And look on Yahweh's face?
See what healing and redemption
What plan you have given up on
For escape, dictated by foreign gods.
Falling into the occults grasp
Although God is able to save
From the burning pit of fire
Will He?
Can He in His justice?
Is it worth it?
To go and find out?

30.

Two worlds, one Earth
Two hates, one people
Killing and maiming
Accusing and ignoring
No one taking blame for violence
Instead seething in ignorant sin
One world bathed in evil
Evil we fought to extinguish
Yet it has returned
The devil in black, marching and saluting
A world that wants to exterminate
In the name of a false messiah.
Another world, to fight the first
Bent on its destruction
Any means seems justified
Their hate is deemed reasonable.
Is this what Yahweh wants?
Justice by any means is not justice
Killing, assaulting, is not purified
Will Yahweh shine down on violence and hate?
By no means!
Let love reign
Let Yahweh rule your hearts.
Let the justice of Heaven's Lamb
Fill our hearts.
That the bringer of sin
The Lord of lies
Who causes such strife,
Will we unite and overcome him?

31.

Darkness comes
To this dying world
Steeped in so much sin
It cannot see to the beyond
Drowning in a world
Without the Son
No one craves the truth
That we hold on to
The darkened sun
Betrays the light
Where we can't be
To live with the One
Yahweh save us
From the dying sun
No one wants truth
To save them all
My heart breaks down
As I cry aloud
For the dearest ones
Who reject the only one
Choices made
To uphold the cross
No flesh is worth
What they've become
Father God deliver me
From the dying sun
So I can breathe
In true tranquility

32.

The blood of Judah's son
Reigns down on all of us
To try and make us see damnation
That we have dug our graves.
Most don't believe in forgiveness
We claim our own salvation
Can our own love find a way?
Is truth something we can make?
Too often the dark sons cry
Out for something like deliverance
Expecting our hands to deliver us
By works and legacies of fathers.
Not even the spirits give us hope
Their misconstrued truths always revealed
Claim logic as our father
But refuse reason and the road it leads.
Yet hope must come
We need it more than ever
Too many are dying in their dreams
Never seeing their legends fruition.
True hope will reveal the lie
That we have come to believe in
Behold! The dawn of awakening
When the Son will find a way.

33.

I will trust in God
My defender
My protector
My friend.
When all others fall around me
By trusting in magic crystals
Or trusting their health to weeds
I will rejoice in your truths.
Far East philosophies
And pagan magics
Have infected the minds of your elect
Until they lose the glory of your salvation.
Deliver me Yahweh from such evil
That pollutes the hearts of apostates
Those that used to be your bride
That have fallen from grace.
You prayed that it would not be possible
But Yahweh, it is happening
The false preachers and teachers
Are leading the flock astray.
They must not have been yours
Never truly giving themselves to you
Trusting too much in this world
Which was created by Your hand.
Bring me to Your glory Yahweh
Let me see Your face
That I will not fall into corruption
That the yeast will not take hold.

34.

Violence becomes your name
As you refuse to protect your own
We give our time, our freedom
And we get abusive behaviour back.
We are the abused, the scorned
The high lords snarl from on top
Refusing to come down.
We put up with injustice
As all they care for is gold
Shining their own crowns
While we unsafely bow to them,
We are the slaves, the forgotten
Although they started like us
We are now forgotten.
Treated like nothing, like dirt
Where is the justice? The support?
Shall we give of ourselves forever?
When the judgement fires come
No one will remember them.
They believe they are gods
Immortal, untouchable
They forget they are flesh
They were born, just like us.
We are the neglected, the nobodies
As we cry to God to save us
To deliver us from this Hell
And know His true freedom.

35.
The lies of the alchemists
Consume the inner spirit
The brothers of the Rosie Cross
Are liars to the ends of the Earth.
Where truth lies in His Word
In the very Logos of God
They strip that truth from our lips
And make magic out of scripture.
Treat them with scorn Oh nations
Let Yahweh sort them out
There is no room in Heavens streets
For their occult philosophies.
We Are the sons of the Most High
The Holy One of Israel
World leaders bow to the secret lies
But we hold our praise for the King.
There is no room for lies on our lips
Only truth will set us free
The Rosie Cross knows all these things
Darkness clouds their thoughts.
Sing praise to the Holy One of Israel
Sing praise to the name of Yahweh
His brothers will rule on golden thrones
To judge the Rosie Crosses deception.
Praise to Him all you cherubim
Praise to Him all you people's
Praise to Him and His truth
Praise the Lord.

36.

Black dreams
Negating our present illusions of
Light
All hope has left
The concert of angels
Expired
Is the song in my heart a ticket
To a present dungeon
Of my own creation?
Stuck in a pit so deep
No end to a torment so
Corrupting
Where can I hope to go
With drawing out sanctified
Bleeding
It drips on an altar
To recognize the
Pain
Need freedom
Can hope return?
Is there something left to believe in?
I truly hope these bonds can break
So that I may gaze on the moon
With gladness and serenity
That I shall not return
To a place of ever induced
Bondage.

37.

The pain,
It's beautiful.
Kind of like a job so masterful.
When it's gone,
Something will be missing,
But the peace to come will be replacing,
Nothing left but to feel,
Feel the blood ever dripping,
To be redeemed by the faithful racing.

Try to wipe the tears away,
But I can't feel the peace, ashamed.
I listen to the preacher, teaching,
Think I'm the one to be blamed.
Know the pearly gates are waiting,
To relieve the stress I'm always feeling.
Try not to force the issue, patiently,
To hear the peaceful choirs of angels singing.

38.
Black leather
Hidden desire
Carnal lusts
Naked dreams
Base depravity
Seek forgiveness
Fall again
Can't escape
The temptation
Clouded eyes
Unseen glory
Defining sin
Reforming minds
Hide myself
Can't confront
Wrongful intentions
Wanting holiness
Performing sin
Lusts power
Controlling minds
Enslaving many
Wrangling youth
Tempting elect
No shelter
All invasive
Need help
Desperately drowning.

39.
Falling tears
Of a broken and fractured soul
Been bound and tied back up
But the cracks have never been mended.
Hurt is so prevalent
Behind the apparent coping
I see the cold coals
Of a fire slowly passing away.
There is hope
Always is
Can breath be sent back to the coals
What words can mend the rents
I ask myself as I look in the
Mirror.
Another time, another place
I felt these same things
Wrote them down to heal
Through black ink
Tears of a new kind
Though I cried, oh I cried.
Can old words on worn parchment
Possibly be the ointment
To mend the scars?

40.
There was once emotion,
I think it was love,
Maybe, in some form,
That I dreamed of.
It was a fair lady,
Strong and tall.
Graceful as the song of birds
In the early hours of morning.
Before the smog of day
Steals away the clean arising breath of air.
Still, I remember that lady, that eros
That made me so ill with grief.
It bled me, a sieve that had no nozzle.
That hopeless dream made me cry out,
To the uncaring day,
People moved, ran by,
With heartless discontent.
As my blood dripped to the crowds,
Bathing them in Levitical servitude,
They ran on by not knowing,
Not caring,
That someone was dying above them.
Slain by eros herself.
I look at her beauty, hoping,
Praying, for her healing touch.
There was none.
Just her joy as she walked off, satisfied.

41.

I bleed out the pain,
In an attempt to feel the same,
As the world which always lies to me,
About how I'm supposed to tell inside.
There is no truth to the claim,
That there is no feeling in the game,
That people play to try to be,
Just to close themselves away and hide.
They try to tell me I'm insane,
That I'm always the one to blame,
For how I feel and fail always to see,
But they never take up to mind,
That there is nothing left to gain,
From those fake flowers in the frame,
Although I just wish to be free,
It'll wait until I'm on the other side.

42.

The rain is falling down
The thunder rings out its glorious sound
There is hope in the storm
The blood cold epiphany that we're all doomed.
What slashes in delicate skin
Will make you believe that we are at an end
The pain isn't a saviour
Yet we please its urges in an attempt at salvation.

Break the seal and pull me to the ground
What hope can come in this hour of night
My enemies come clambering to me
Hoping to see me fall, to see me die
It's all come to this
I don't know what to say to make it end
There's so much sin in the day
Yet they all point at me saying I'm the one to blame.

The storm is the new tell all
Who will terrorize themselves in their flesh
Rather than turn to a true hope
That has the only real chance at saving them
Will the world bath in Yahweh's light
Or drown in their own blood and strife
Watch them come at Hell's front gate
We are the silence that condemns them all.

43.

Blackened this heart of mine
To keep it truly hidden away
Been hurt so much it's time
To protect my source of pain.
My flesh is weak so I cannot take
Why it took you so long to see
That I am worth something more
Then all the blood I tend to leak.
Agony is this world to me
A golden gate I truly hoped for
Can Yahweh relieve the pain
Through grace I cannot feel.
I know my pain has been paid for
But I feel like I'm being crucified
Though Yahweh paid the price
Still feel like I'm being punished.
Save me, Yahweh God
Before I once again brand my flesh
To relieve the persecution
Of being truthful to you.
Take the blood that falls from me
Heal the wound that forever bleeds
Restore my darkened heart
Sanctify me, my Lord and God.

44. Blood Drips

Blood drips onto the floor
Into crevices of the stained hardwood
Adding iron red to the dark color
I wait for the darkness to come
Take me away.
To die is gain, but to live is Christ
Yet I find it so
Hard.
Can I know the bonds I force myself into each day
Be finally broken?
So many needs for life that it causes so much unneeded
Stress.
If I can find freedom some way somehow
I will welcome it
For now, I will wait as
The blood drips onto the floor
Hurting myself.

45. Daughter Nation
Promiscuous nation
Like an errant daughter abandoning
Her fealty
Our home invaded by sins
That have no interest in purity
The daughter is used
And cast away
Yet she goes to the next nation
Whoring.
She has become the harlot of nations
Can the heart, her church
Stand?
Take back her honor
Return her to her first true love?
Turn compassion
Into forgiveness
Can her father take her back
To restore her to queendom?
To her royal throne?
Where she can be just and
Pure?
Where is hope?
Where is
Justice?

46. Detestable Things

You will see more detestable things,
The earth cries out for the
Murder,
And blood we cast on its soil
Seeping with ages of sin
In its depths
The devil desires we cradle
In the mountains grip
That tell of our total depravity.

You will see more detestable things,
Dispensational lies give us false hope's
Watching skies for a false
Rapture
Not spoken of in the word
Chosen Abrahamic seed
Hope in false prophecies
Leading masses to eternal flame
Is there desire to know the truth?

You will see more detestable things,
We throw away into careless coffers
Being lousy stewards as we
Gamble
Thinking just once more
My greed will answer me
But there is no hope
No salvation
Where we put our hearts
The line to sulphur grows
As we cut ourselves to call on
False gods.

You will see more detestable things,
When Eros and Cupid
Seduce

Our kids to become parents
All due to erotic gratification
Loss of
Self-control
As we lust after people
To objectify them
As items to be used
Rather than to feel
Agape
Towards the forlorn

You will see more detestable things,
Casting spells while chanting incantations for
Witchcraft
The occult bleeds deception
To those crying for fulfillment
But leaving them empty
Craving more power
Empty batteries, eating souls
Burning bridges to false
Heavens
Assuming they can be united to God

You will see more detestable things,
Communicating with the dead but really
Demons
Telling us lies and false
Prophecies
We are desperate to believe
Unclean spirits leading us astray
While we believe that the dead realm
Hold answers and hidden
Secrets
Spit in the face of Yahweh
To see into the future
Only He knows

You will see more detestable things,

Liquid spirits cause us to lose control
While we give in to deviant
Intoxication
Is the poison worth condemnation?
Why cloud judgement
So we can champion drunkenness
Laugh at glorified stories of
Debauchery
Dumbing down our own minds

You will see more detestable things,
Taking up the green, cold the
High
Believing it is good for us
But it brings about chemical change
We are willing to alter ourselves for
Gateway to more powerful
Narcotics
Ending up in detox
All for a laugh
The constant giggle
Enslaving our minds
Addicting body and soul
To an intoxicating bud.

47. Forgotten Stable

Blazing throne
Of glory unbeholden
Though we speak
Of love
Too often judgement finds us.
Can our sins be forgiven?
Do we deserve Yahweh's trust?
Black kids
Shot in the streets
For nothing other than fear
Misunderstanding.
Anger towards
Innocence,
Lost in translation.
Youth disrespecting,
Their uncaring parents.
Try to pass blame,
Someone else's fault.
Cross, blazing in holy fire
Justice can and will come.
We will not be
Forgotten forever.
Hope lies over the
Horizons fire.
In a Davidic town
Where a stable lies
Forgotten.

48. Freedom

Reverberating chords hammer
Out a song with offensive
Yet soothing roars of vocals
By false messiah like Slipknot
Or other European death metal acts.
Regardless a certain amount of
Saddened comfort seeps into
A mind clouded with a barren and wasteland
Of grief and pain.
While many try to reach into
The Abyss to pull me out
What can there be up in the world
Of another false messiah that pretends
To live in Yahweh's light.
They twang and spoken poetry
To masses craving to define themselves
Though I live in a self-help
Inflicted Sheol, there is peace
As I know who I am, what
I am defined as in this place.
I do not
Cannot
Live away from the screams of my serenity
Though you may not
Understand
The joy I find here
It comes with pain and fear
But it also comes with the pill,
The antidote,
Where the "light" above drowns in
Alcohol.
Freedom is a lie up there,
I live free,
I live in peace.

49. Our Example

We sit in humble temples, while rulers of the world
Try to come against us, in action and in word.
Waving a flag of peace, we quietly march along
While the worlds at war around us, do we dare day it's wrong?
Electing evil people, into kinghood's grand seat
Singing out his praises, while hunger grovels at his feet.
Suffering gets a backbenched seat, while the arms of war extend
To cause more hurt and fallen tears, and never will it end.
People of God rise up to claim what is right, just and pure
Set an example they cannot ignore, and Christ will win for sure.

50. Poltergeist

Secluded walls containing evil
Breaking a month that doesn't understand
Bound to a place of forgotten love
Where blood may shed by the end.
Howling wails fill the starless night
Fragile mind cannot bear the thought
Battle of wills with unseen powers
To overcome misguided security.
Floating objects add to the will
That surround the forsaken home
Sides of light desire to defeat
But the creeping darkness ever overcomes.
As innocent flesh approaches this realm
Unprepared for such a dominant mind
To be repelled the final outcome
One will conquer, the other will die.

51. Right Road

Came across a fork in the
Road
Signs were confusing, unintelligible.
One split felt warm and cozy
A banana delicacy dressed in lots of toppings
To please succulent souls.
This way I knew was truth
The way a child believes every word you
Speak.
Even if they find it strange
To them it is truth because their
Uncle told them and he isn't wrong.
Or Sunday School teachers who don't want to be
Challenged.
Kids are too young to anyway but they try.
Truth is something they want
And they trust you to have it.
The fork though
It is
Evil.
Cold and relentless.
A dark form moving in the background,
There is no truth here,
Just lies.
The devil himself
Is down this road.
The pull nags us.
We want it.
The evil, the brutality.
Try to take one step towards the light,
But surprised to find myself going down the
Wide road
The wrong road.
Truth verses lies yet I choose the deception.
I know better,
Don't I?

At least I thought I did.
Yet down the right road I go.
This is the right road, isn't It?

52. Salvation

Black fires burn
The crimson heart of secular
Philosophy and dreams.
Hope drained from effervescent
Cones of caffeine.
We fight for what
We think we know
But no one really knows.
Children fight and play
In streets flooding
With a thick crimson flow.
Yet we ignore the
Fiery tide of desire
Because there's nothing,
Nothing but hollow desires
Spilt like water
Growing nothing but weeds.
Yahweh warned us, yet
Still, we follow our own hearts,
The anchor doesn't exist
Yet we throw it overboard
Hoping to save ourselves.
Hoping, for salvation.

53. Self-Help

A spirit consumes us
Even though we try to deny it
Religion is a façade to our thinking
Yet publishers make millions on books to self improve the soul

Is there something we're missing out on?
What salvation are we yearning for?
Is humanity God now
That we've given up the thought of true freedom

Help isn't something we really want
Just a catalyst to justify the great perversion
Of Gnostic thought we are slaves to
Denial, here comes denial

It's all around
Differential equations on life
That confuse us that are
Trying to figure this all out

Is Yahweh just a foxhole
Way of thinking
To bail us out like some failed car company
To not take any responsibility

For our errant thinking
That we have it all down pat
Like a chart we graph out
To make it look like it all makes sense

Yet it doesn't and we
Know the lie in front of us
Just choosing to ignore it
So we won't be responsible

When the fires come

For the justification of err'd saints
Does the pope not give a damn
When the world falls apart?

Yet we buy the books to save
Our precious sense of self
Not accepting the true thought
Of what truly justifies

Sanctifies to make pure
Hearts that yearn for peace
That next self-help book will tell me
It has to tell me

54. Tears

Black clouds
Form in the sky above me
And the rain begins to trickle
Down the dirty glass window.
I reach out
To touch the pane
But hold back as the fear
Makes me,
Hesitate.
I don't know why but
Anxiety is the song
That my heart sings.
Operatic,
Like an old victorious Viking
Drunk on the blood of war.
Like the rain,
Tears fall
Watering the plants
On the windowsill.
At least someone feels,
Life,
Even if it is salty and stained
With blood from the vampiric
Reality of my fear.

55. The Curtain
Do I dare remember the velvet sheet,
That separates truth from myth?
The creature within with crimson eyes,
Which speak to humanity's infidelity?
The tentacled limbs with dagger truths,
And breath that smells of death,
The worm like way it moved to and fro,
To reach out for my flesh.
Its skin of stone yet soft as sludge,
Sent shivers to my soul,
"What soul," did it ask, "Do you think you have,
That I would not claim for my own?"
Then I saw the end of man,
Come down in a fiery blaze,
As ancient creatures arose from the depths,
Forgotten by all but themselves.
No sights of salvation, only condemnation,
As multitudes are fed to its maw,
The sun doesn't shine on such despair,
It only hides its saving grace.
Should I remember the sights,
And warn those who dare enough to listen?
No,
Wait,
The curtain,
Do not look behind the curtain!

56. The Door
Ancient portal circled in enigmatic stone
Granting access to oldened ways that only
Elder beings of both good and evil reside.
We think the door is a gateway to a stairway
Leading to heaven or hell but the truth is more
Subtle
An old man's library where secrets are hidden
The elder human holds the secrets of the universe
This apostle, undying
John
He cries over the state of the world and the desire
To see us learn beyond the door.

57. The Tempter

Nightmares, scratching,
Invading,
Demeaning.
Burning soul like eyes,
Penetrating,
Discovering.
Seductive voices,
Brainwashing,
Relearning.
Unclean thoughts,
Gaining,
Corrupting.
Temptations, implanted,
Drawing,
Breathing.
Self-destruction ensued,
Scarring,
Bleeding.

Chapter 3: The Judgment

58. Prophet of the End

In blissful sleep on quiet night
   The blessed chosen slept
   Dreaming dreams of joy and glee
With no shadows in the skyline
But the dreams did change in screaming horror
And the chosen one tries to wake
A man appears in tar black robes
Holding out a rough-hewn hand
"Fear not my chosen for I am he
Who sets all things aright
 What you will see will come to pass
In the future all too soon."
The dream then changes, the chosen screams
As the day turns into night
Fires blaze all around,
The dream is then consumed
A city without a precious name
Sits red in the horizon
As he approaches, he quickly sees
The buildings charred and black
The chosen asks, "What is this
That I should see this end?
This world I thought was immortal
Should die so easily?"
"Do not be fooled this world will feel
The angered fires of Hell."
The man this spoke as a tear formed
And trickled down his face
The chosen sees the gentle tear
And asks in angered haste
"Who are you that you would condone
Such needless suffering?"
"I am that I am, I cannot change
This is shown to you for you to warn

If people turn from corrupt ways
The tide will be withheld
That is your task, do you not see?
To tell of this event
Your gentle heart has spoken loud
In all of Heaven's courts."
The chosen sighed and looked around
At all the broken homes
Forgotten dreams and fragile hearts
Consumed in holy wrath
"This task is mine, I cannot refuse."
The humble chosen spoke
The black robed man smiled in joy
At the humble, tearful acceptance
"Then off with you, to the real world
May you never forget all this."
"I doubt I will, how can I forget
Such fury before my sight."
Then the chosen awoke in his room
Empty and alone
This prophet knew he must begin
Or all will see their dooms.

59.
Whispers filling up the mind
Causing thoughts to fall away
Filled by empty feelings of doubt
Causing sober mental strains.
Objects moving without strings
To taunt unexpected guests
Repressing memory in hopes to forget
The horrors that lay within.
Nightmares fill haunted dreams
That promise angry fulfillment
Depicting pictures of bloody horror
To unexpected fragile visions.
Names carved in door posts
Of those submitted to die
Fulfilling these deeds in gruesome turns
Each spirit calling its due.
Vengeance consumes ethereal hearts
For wrongs in distant pasts
Ever forgetting corrected sins
Crimson ink writing its significance.

60.
Claim innocence
But your actions speak
Lies and debauchery all around
Making that a blanket of solace.
Say you are good
Deserving of salvation
Yet deny He who authored such grace
You give heed to false prophets.
Sit in a pew to feel good, unconvicted
Buried alive in your own sin
You will all be judged
Your blasphemies will not stand.
Oh nation, I mourn for your soul
A power has arisen
To be an arm of judgement
Your own sins have brought this on you.
Adultery a daily occurrence
With the whore of Babylon
The bride herself feeling the price of iniquity
Being judged for not taking a stand.
Allowing unclean spirits to cry out in our synagogues
Ulcers of greed emerging
Wanting all for yourself
Running the devils' race.
Hoping the Saviour will pick you up
Not living in fear
The day will come when Zion bleeds
Because you focus only on yourself
While forgetting the truth.

61.

Cry out for justice
As defined by Your own mind
A road with Yahweh
Leading to self-destruction.
No one is capable of true good
All pervading good
That changes lives and restores souls
So convinced you have earned heaven
While denying God and falling to Hell.
Destined for flame
Refusing to bow
Self-godhood consuming all
Yet no one is good
No not one.
Absent light that is quashed
Every time truth is heard
So desperate to dowse holy fire
And spit in the face of Yahweh.
Yet you call yourself good?
Put down others
Deceive, lie, steal,
Act as whitewashed graves
Elegant to look at
Yet worms eat you from the inside.
Kneel before Christ
Accept His grace
Be reconciled in His love
Sin's stain to be removed
And live in joy.

62.

Bride of Christ
Light to the world
Do you not comprehend the times?
Judgement has come!
Yet you are blind
Yet you are deaf
False prophets and false teachers
Pollute your minds
Telling you what you want to hear.
The bride will be judged first
Before the coming of the lawless one
After which Christ will reign.
We are not ready
May God delay His hand of justice
To allow us more time
Weep! Wail oh children of the Lamb!
Can Yahweh stay His hand forever?
A mountain of sin mocks Zion
As you serve your own desires first
Drunkards and adulterers fill our pews.
Yet there is no one to hold them to account
Fear God's holiness
Can you stand faultless before Yahweh?
No one can!
The bride must be purified
Before the world sees her king
After the darkness comes
To shed guilty blood.

63.
Opening the door to the hangman
When we appeal to ourselves
Willingly walk to the gallows
By igniting our own pride.
Lust, greed, and self-indulgence
All end at the hangman
Who will wrap the rope around your neck
And laugh when the trap gives way?
The devil's hangman shows no mercy
He doesn't care about your wealth
Your looks or attitude are grains of sand
Worthless to him yet we try to pay.
Laughter as the rope goes taut
As we plead to the end
Thinking we can save ourselves
But the hangman does not serve us.
Sheol is his master
The grave that descends to the Abyss
Given a ticket to kill
Written by our own hands.
Only Yahweh's righteousness can save
Before we open the door to the hangman.

64.

Can you extend your life by one day?
Yahweh gives us life
By His word we are sustained
The chaotic powers of the grave
Hold no power over us
When the Holy One speaks our doom.
Yet you praise the fruits of His hand
As gods that will usurp Yahweh's will
Believing plants from the sinful ground
Can rise you up above the Almighty?
The Accuser was thrown down
Trying to raise himself above Yahweh.
Wicked generation!
Will your pact with Sheol
Spare you from the rod of His wrath?
Can you be ever wasting away
While deteriorating in your own filth?
Only by His hand are you saved
Yahweh gives us life.
Yahweh gives salvation.
Embrace His covenant
Loose yourself from death's treaty
And know true freedom!

65.
Ten plagues, bringing gods to their knees
A true God, making the Nile bleed
Have always tried to enslave the Holy people
Whether a Sea of Reeds or a tank blast.
Machine Gun Majesty
Hours bleeds, Ra darkness
Pair is gods and Isis is debased
The gods of the sand are blown away
Forced to bow to Yahweh whom they deny.
Machine Gun Majesty
They can't stand before His grace
Forced out of Heaven to be displaced
Deceive making and be condemned
Yet grace will reign with none to contend.
Machine Gun Majesty
The final war will bathe Thebes in fire
No apostate nation left to defend
Gunfire with the sun's fire
Their gods will bleed in the end.
Machine Gun Majesty

66.
Build iron gods and drop to them
Your knees scraped bare and bleeding
Give praise to the work of your hands
With no power to save anything.
Yet flesh will come to these old bones
Yahweh will breathe new life on us
An awakening will occur
When the judges return to our cursed world.
There is promise in the suffering
Even when we bow to our false gods
While we bite the hand that feeds us
Fall down, repent and see the true Son.
Feel the fire of judgement come
Eventually Magog will invade us
And be forced to serve a foreign god-king.
Hear the call of Yahweh
Be freed forever by His love
Receive the new life offered to all
And know peace, no longer fear.

67.

Now we draw the battle lines
In blood and sand in all its kind
The Shadow grows in our empathy
Until the scars are too late to see.

Until this war is over
I'll never lose my way
Wait it out until the end of days

Misanthropic lives I crave
It's hard to believe we can be saved
The earth speaks against its pain
Blood we spilled won't be washed by rain.

While we die
Breaking out all our hate
While we kill
The judgement fires, burn away
Our conscious minds, unafraid

Rising beasts, that claim from us
All the ghosts where we put our trust
Our blackest sins, condemning us too
Ignorant minds, polluting us right through

Taint, our bleeding souls
Denying all the truth we're told
Bite down on the maker's hand
I guess it's plain we'll never understand.

68.

You were reared up
Brought up as holy children
A birthright handed to you by Yahweh
But you forsook the covenant
Rejected your true Davidic king
The God and man, Jesus
Israel, Israel
How I mourn for you
You were chosen
The splendour of Yahweh's crown
Yet you chose dirt and apostasy
You chose to eat with pigs
Then at the Kings table
A day is coming
When you will be forced to choose
Between Jesus and the lawless one
There will be no forgiveness
For the final rejection
Of the one who raised you as brothers
The grafted in branch
Gentiles all
Will receive your due blessings
Until you renounce your sin
Return to your King
Oh, apostate Ariel!
So that your covenant can be renewed
And once again be the glory of your King!

69.

When stress overcomes a weary soul
A demon lord awaits in the thickets
To pounce and demand covenant blood
From your own flesh.
My flesh is a testament to the power
Of the one called by the name: Cybele.
Messenger of Satan
That pulls so many to the Abyss
As blades and guns carve up flesh
For the demons' consumption,
Free yourselves!
By Yahweh's power
I renounce the demon now!
May you burn in the bowels of the Abyss
Until judgement comes for you
Hurt not those who do not know
Who do not see or hear
Let Yahweh's light touch them
That we may all be free
From this painful addiction
That never more may we feed our blood
To anyone or thing.
God has not asked for this
Nor has it entered His mind.
So, let us live in the freedom of Yahweh's love
So, judgement may fall on Cybele's head.
May no tear fall from my eyes
Until the day comes
When Yahweh calls me home.

70.
Father of all the heavens
Ruler of the earth and sky
God of all creation
I ask you to free my mind
From the power of Concord and Discord
Of fake peace and chaos
By the blood of the first Son
The one we call Jesus,
Yahweh free me from the demonic grip
These spirits have put on me
Claiming parts of my spirit
To hold me in bondage
By the power of Christ
Freedom can be known
And bondage of the unclean
To be sent to the Abyss
Blood from the cross pour over me
That freedom may be known
No powers of darkness to claim me
Only love to eternally bless me.

71.

Destiny to suffer
Should we let them decide?
Separate themselves
To the evil innard desires
To face the Great Tribulation
That they may know the pain of sin
Can they repent
To turn to the Holy One?
Even in their own tribulations
There is no repentance
Preferring to let hard, cold blood
Dribble down their throats.
There is no redemption
No faith
Shall we let them face the Great Tribulation
And the lawless one be their god?
Since they pursue their Gnostic science
Will the false christ reveal himself to them?
That Aeon they pursue to know
Through math and physics
Shall they wait until the tribulation?
To finally see the work of their hands?
When the Holy One of Israel
Will finally show His glory?
I pray they will not meet this fate
Though friendships be lost
Though family be severed
I ask that they will be found.

72.
Wisdom
A concept so hard to grasp
Shall we reason under the grave sun?
Will thunder consume our thoughts?
Unlikely.
Solomon was the wisest
Given such insight by Yahweh
All came from the nations
To mighty Israel
To learn from the blessed king
Hand chosen by Yahweh
Writing books of scripture
While teaching the world.
Such topics as modern science
No one questioned him
Even legal cases decided by reason
To split a child in two
The true mother then speaks.
Yet our wise men today
Throw away the fact of reason
Calling it pagan.
Did Solomon not show reason?
Did he not teach it to all who came?
That being all nations that heard?
Foolish philosopher kings
The wisdom of Yahweh
Lights up your foolish thoughts.

73.

Secret lies we crave to find
In Gnostic halls all forlorn
We act as though they are saved
Not realizing we'll all burn in Hell.
God's truth is all revealed
No secret halls hiding tomes
The only mysteries are ever lies
Told by the father of darkness.
Magic rites we believe will save
What happened to simple faith?
Why sell the soul for a blood drip?
When holy blood bought us all.
Expose the lies the Masons tell
And save yourselves from Hades
The road to perdition is paved with gold
To seduce you ever after.
See Yahweh's light in the sky
Be free by faith to believe
God has not hidden himself in secret halls
Or dealt with fire to consume.
Accept the cross and be renewed
The only mystery now revealed
That Christ is king over all the world
Even Gnostic Aeons bend their knee.
See the truth Yahweh has shown
And free yourself from Hell.
There are no secrets in God's love
We all are with him in his hand.

74.

Heeding Yahweh's call
To engage with the heretics
That run this world
Under the angel of light.
We are enslaved
To a cruel machine
That drives us to depravity
All for debased entertainment.
Heeding Yahweh's call
To burn away the Gnostic
There is no hope left
That this world willingly offers.
We are the lost ones
The brothers of the Christ child
To bring light back
Before the candle is snuffed out.
Heeding Yahweh's call
To counter the fanatic
We battle forces we cannot see
Drawing up the battle lines.
Brandish our swords of truth
To fight back the ever night
Before the dark one comes
And we are all called home.

75.
I will be the watchman
When friends falter before Yahweh
To pursue occult philosophies
And believe in false magics.
When they claim they follow You
And obey Your commandments
Hunger for the truth of Your Word
Yet the truth of their depravity is open.
I will be the watchman
To the family that mix their potions
Claiming they are helping
Yet neglecting truthful medicines.
When they criticize me for speaking truth
Yet the lie is evident in their life
When they want emotional freedom
Thinking it contained in a bottle.
I will be the watchman
To a world steeped in sin
If I don't speak out, who will?
Their blood will not be on my hands.
When I give an account to Yahweh
About my time in this place
I will not let their guilt condemn me
Or their sin send me to Tartarus.

76.

Yahweh commanded, I obeyed
A close friend gone
Fallen to the Abyss
Believing in and furthering enemy philosophies
So, a decision had to be made
My soul for theirs?
My goal is in Heaven
To sing before the holy throne.
She says she wants the same
Then preaches magical teachings.
You cannot serve two masters
She's become a witch doctor
Forcing unregistered medicine at people
Been warned twice
As the Bible commands
And both warnings rejected.
Just as Paul wrote to Titus
To cast these people out of your life
So, I have done with her.
Forgive me Father
For not doing so earlier
I wanted to believe she'd repent
But the fires of Hell have consumed her.
She's in your hands now
Do with her
As her sins deserve.

77.

Lining up against the storm
Dragon warriors waiting to crush
The fighters defending the light
Evil men of blackened steel
Seeking the end of truth
A great Spirit, the Comforter
Soars above the side of light
While a great demon of old
In the form of dragons' fire
Waits behind the black lines
Disciplined, the great columns move forth
Jerusalem and Gog go for war
The monster from the pit
Looking to rule in Yahweh's stead
While the armies of redeemed heirs
Seek to preserve the reign of their king
The Lion of Judah speaks
Fire rains down from the sky
Incinerating the armies of the lawless one
The dragon bound forever throw into a lake
A lake of burning sulphur there to eternally die
That the Lamb may reign in Judah forever.

78. Lament Against Parliament

Oh, house of northern lords
Do you not see the trouble in the land?
Do you not hear the cries of the voiceless?
Do you not smell the gout in your hearts?
You do not see or hear the plight of the people
The gout you smell you blame on the nation
Your nation founded under God that you abhor
Repent foolish leaders. Repent for the day of the Lord is near!
Do you not think that Yahweh won't rise up a scepter
Born of his very wrath that cries for justice?
As Israel of old was punished by their God, Yahweh
Beware before He punishes us!
Before He sends foreign nations against us,
To dash our warriors against the rocks,
Before false teachers continue to lead us astray
And lead our youth to unfortunate ends!
Our nation is sick, cry out to Yahweh that He will heal us!
His mercy knows no bounds,
He is willing to graft back in a lost branch.
Cry out His name before all hope is lost,
Before the nations of the North overcome us all.

79. Lost Glory
I watched the glory leave the temple,
There were no tears,
No grief.
Sin encompassed all minds,
No regret, just ecstasy.
Jealousy
The idol
Worshipped by the masses,
They shed tears for
Tammuz
But not for the loss of their Lord.

I watched the glory leave the temple,
Fertility and bunnies,
Chocolate and all
Bloody extremities.
Blood drips like water from a
Fountain.
Yet they don't care,
Their God is gone,
Gnostic philosophy replacing theology.

I watched the glory leave the temple.

80. Sulphur

People left wanting
River of life,
Trickle of peace,
Soothing, relaxing,
Picnic on the shore,
Children playing,
Young lovers, frolicking
Flowing
Through the ultimate judgement seat.
Tears falling
Watching the sulphur lake
Line of people left to dive
Gift of love
Forsaken
Trees of the garden,
Apple's, oranges, bananas
All left behind
The look of pain,
Tracks in the asphalt,
Lines in the sand,
Crevices in the rock face,
Chiseled on burrowed faces.
Gentle rain,
Drizzling,
Soothing, sleeping
Evaporated by the fire.
Yet the line continues
Onward.

81. The Irishman

Critics me for rushing out of work
Yet you act like the place is torture for you
As though your soul is being forfeit by being there
Your own salvation will send you to the pit
Arrogance
Pride
Brown-nosing
All things you think are worth spending work time on
Will see you to the grave
Getting drunk at the bar
Coming to work the next day
Act like the hangover is our fault
Grow up
You're a father
Act like a child
You try to take a buy out
Do you really think you're worth two million dollars?
The first place you head when you get to work is the managers office
Haven't even timed in yet and you're already
Kissing butt
Get your alcoholic and poisonous thinking out of here
We'll be better for it

Chapter 4: The Hope

82.

Glory to God in the highest
For He has shown his wondrous might
Though I suffer in this place
He has not left me out of His reach.
The wicked succeed around me
While I struggle to make it through each day
But your praise is always on my lips
My soul longs and aches for your healing touch.
How long Justin cry out to You?
My voice has nearly reached its limit
My heart continues to groan
But your eyes fall on the afflicted.
Your sit on your throne in heaven
In all things your word is law
So, I will praise you with broken lips
While my heart gets filled anew.
Do not forget your promise O God
To restore me to your throne
Show your face to the righteous
So the wicked will know their final judgement.

83.
Open my eyes, my Lord
At the start of each day
To see your glory in the skies
That will drive me to my knees
Give me words to pray I ask
To please your loving heart
Not my will, but yours be done
Is what I want to see
Foolish needs sometimes come forth
Yet you hear me so I rejoice
Bring me to your holy side
So, I can sigh in relief
And praise your name forevermore
In Heavens golden streets
Draw me close, don't let me go
My God, I ask of thee

84.
Though it be a reflection of your hand
The earth itself does not compare to you
Creation itself cries out to You
It longs for the day you will come to claim it.
Sins shadow covers it for a time
But your light will chase away the darkness
Though that darkness assails your garden
You remain vigilant by Your Word.
By your Word mountains tremble
By your Word life begins
You remain truthful to your precepts
And are trustworthy in your thoughts.
No power may stand before You
That you have not ordained to be
O Lord God, continue in your love and power
May your name be spoken on every tongue.
Your testament will stand forever and ever
As will your unending and unfailing love.

85.
Sing to the Lord all you nations
Dance all you people to His praise
Give of your heart for His graces
Sing to the Lord, your voices raise.
We live in the shadow of his coming
Living by His light in our hearts
Joy comes with every morning
The sorrow flees away for now.
Celebrate people for freedom given
Do not be ashamed to sing His name
Offer gifts That are freely given
Let His name in countries sing.
Though we're assaulted for His name
He reaches down to protect us
We need not fear the fleeing darkness
Since we have security in His name.

86.
Sanctify me O God
Make me as holy as you are
I am but clay in your mighty hands
Hold me to your image and purpose.
Though I stray off the path
You draw me back into your sanctum
Purify my heart my Lord,
Let sun not gain a foothold here.
Though the days seem long and dark
Your holiness shines hope in life
Because of your sacrifice
I can stand blameless in your sight.
Always keep your hand on me
So that I may learn your ways
Draw me into your inner courts
So that I may know you like a brother.
Engrave your word on my heart
So that I may know your mighty will
Make me holy, O Lord,
As I praise your holy name.

87.

Mighty is God who rules in Zion
No shadow can hide from His face
How foolish we are to build more Babel's
To try and unseat Him from His throne.
Must He throw us into confusion
Once more to show us the way?
Yet He has shown us the way
And it is most perfect.
Joy and righteousness are ours to claim
If we look up and see His face
He smiles on us in all things
His wings protect us from our enemies.
How long do we think we can stand
Without His arm of power
To sustain us in our ignorance?
Yet He sustains us still with love.
How many towers will we strive to build
To rival Heaven's throne?
Do we not see He cannot be matched?
Yet we try with all our might.
Bend your knee and give praise to Him
You wicked, twisted men
For He is full of honor and power
And these are owed to Him.

88.

Lord of all creation
Your glory shines in all things
Nature itself is evidence of your hand
So no one has an excuse.
Your glory is like water
That quenches the driest thirst
It is nectar that sustains me
It holds me upright in all I do.
Show your love and glory through me
May I be an outlet for your power
So all who are around me can see your love
And know that you are God.
May the wicked say, "He is blessed!"
And as hungry children wish for that blessing
Make your power evident in me
So all will know your blessing.
Shine through me, O Lord,
Let your light touch the darkness
May the candle of your love
Illuminate the darkest of rooms.
Call me close to you
So that I can see your face
Let you be my only desire
Since you are all that satisfies.
May the peoples now before you
As they see your power in me
Write your law on my heart
So I may walk in righteousness.

89.
Lord our Lord, your hand is in all I see
Your breath of life whispers through the trees.
By your will children grow and learn to thrive
You extend your graces to young and old.
Life you have given and always sustain
Rejoicing in your power is our praise.
Though at times I feel weak
You pick me up and carry me on.
You don't let us give up or fail
Because you will us onward.
See the beauty of this marvelous world
How good was your voice to speak it into being.
Beauty abounds in things big and small
From the hares' small face to the mighty oak.
You reach out your hand to display your glory
Blessed be your name, O Lord
In life and beauty, you are here
And I will forever praise your mighty name.

90.
The fire won't reign forever.
One day Yahweh's glory will shine
Spend too much time on insignificant things
Polluting our minds, consuming our thoughts.
Agents of the Abyss call us fools
For focusing on the flame
Of our own desires
To ease pain we cause ourselves.
The fire won't reign forever.
It will be thrown into burning sulphur
We will rise, Yahweh's chosen children
To judge the living and the dead.
Those that condemn us
Will fall away to Gehenna
Into a realm of everlasting night and burning
To be bound and never find relief.
The fire won't reign forever.
As Christ arose so we will receive new flesh
A restored image that no one can corrupt
Each with a secret name known only by the Lamb.
David's throne will be established on Earth
In the New Jerusalem we will find peace
No more anger, no more tears
We will rise and finally see the face of God.

91.

Unceasing grace, our deepest need
Called to an unyielding live
Though we try to master our own destinies
To be human means to love.
Grasp the light, make us whole
Songs of angels resound in our hearts
"Holy, holy is Yahweh Almighty."
Even the rocks cry out.
To be touched with intimacy
We could never know elsewhere
Enfolded in acceptance
Never being turned away.
Arrogant people, out for gratification
When what we want is kindness
It waits beside us
Just reach out, touch it.
Build us anew, to be whole
In ways we only dreamed
Living life as it was meant to be
Yahweh, take me!
Take me to where I belong.

92.
Come to the shadow of Zion's hill
Where the beacon of hope reigns
A chosen people to show Yahweh's grace
To touch all of us and give us peace.
We will find security on Zion's hill
The prophets voice still rings there
Judges of old pass down their wisdom
That we may know unfailing grace.
Fear the one who reigns on Zion's hill
For He will come in glory
To bring the ruler of this world
Down to his pathetic, undeserving knees.
We will find peace on Zion's hill
All tears will be wiped away
Sin will no longer make us feel disgrace
We will be true children of the Holy One.
Come now all, to Zion's hill.

93.
Confusion runs against the grain
As I sit and pray for rain
Wash away the sorrows that I hold
To hope one day I can be bold
With a scream of silence
For everyone who escaped the pain
When there's nothing left to gain
As we plead so hard for repentance
And when the stories fully told
And God himself in His arms I hold
As the heart of love beats out my name
To realize I'm not the same
And all the tears I feel
With those times I feel I should fold
At the heart of grace washes away the cold
To realize a life that's real

94.
You lift me when I fall
And bring light from darkness
You are the testimony of creation
Your Spirit holds back the encroaching darkness.
I crave your truth when I rise
I cannot help but ponder your Word
Creation speaks of your glory
You make weakness your strength.
The stars sing your praises
Galaxies are formed by Your might
Your voice resonates with power
Yet is gentle enough for the soul.
You redeem from the sinful and wretched
To make your holiness shine
You heal broken spirits
That we may live free from pain.
Only by glorifying you can we know freedom
Sin cannot enslave us anymore
The Lion of Judah,
A lamb that was slain.
The prophets longed to see these days
When your Spirit is poured out
You push back the gates of Hell
That we may be free, evermore.

95.
My enemies flourish against me
My foes spread deceit about me
Their bows bend towards me
Swords sharpened to my skin.
Bring me to the altar of Yahweh!
Bring your accusations against me!
What wrong have I done?
What derision have I caused?
If any of this is true
Let the fires of Carmel consume me
If Yahweh has not forgiven me
Let my head descend to Sheol.
But you Oh Yahweh are my shield
You scatter my foes before me
Your song fills me with gladness
Your voice soothes my soul.
My enemies are forced to kneel before you
In that day of judgement, I will be vindicated
You will lift me up to Heaven
To your holy temple.
My foes will acknowledge you are God
They will affirm that I have done no wrong
Yahweh, you are my deliverer
Holy Spirit, my Comforter.
I sleep peacefully in your presence
My soul brought to your rest
The Sabbath dawns on the horizon
And I am filled with your peace.

96.
What kind of faith can it take
To see even the back of Yahweh?
Moses asked to see your face
But your glory was too holy
None could look on you and live.
Now that the price is paid,
The blood spilt,
The curtain torn,
Can I be able to gaze upon
Your holiness?
I crave to know you as Moses did,
The apostles too
That I may walk the path of those great men of
Faith.
Only you are capable of such mercies.
I pray that I can see your glory
Before I die.
Not that I need to see you to believe
For blessed are those who do not see yet believe,
But just to have the faith to know
That I need not fear the wrath of your glory.
You are too holy for me
Wretched human that I am.
I cannot go a day without failing
To live up to your standard.
Yet I crave your holiness
In my life, to see that in that glory
There is grace,
And love.

97.

I live in the night
The glorious absence of the sun
Some say it is not natural
That we should live in the day
Absorb critical nutrients
From the rays of light
But
It makes me uncomfortable
Did Yahweh not bless both
Day and Night?
Did He not call both Good?
Though I prefer darkness
I do not live in darkness
Do not confuse the two
Where devils frolic and demons play
Is not where I call home
Light must shine in the dark
But I am of the light
Of the blood of Yahweh
Too many think the night
Is akin to demonic dark
But it is not
This is not the haunt of Babylon
Ruins where unclean spirits
Torment the light of truth
I am not unclean for preferring the light of the moon
Just a soul that finds solace under the stars.

98.

Your hand created the mightiest of heavens,
But oh Lord, you come down to judge the sinner.
None can stand before your fires of wrath
Even your Son desired to call down heavenly inferno
Upon the children of sinful Israel.
You are just in your ways, and none are worthy before you.
But Yahweh God, you have us a way
Through the blood of the chosen Messiah
Who hung on a cross to bear down on his brokenness
All the fury of your outstretched arm.
The sky darkened at the display of wrath
Against yourself, your very flesh
So that you could go back to Heaven,
As the true Holy One of Israel,
To judge the living and the dead.
None can stand before you
Except by the power of your mercy.
You are righteous in all you do,
There is no wrongness in your being.
We are called to fear you, Oh Lord.
Your holiness and goodness is so vast
We cannot fathom it.
Those of us that do not submit to Your rule
Will pay the ultimate price.
Bring Your kingdom to Earth,
Let the shining hope of the nations,
Christ,
Rule from Your holy city.
That all people will know once and for all,
That You are God.

99.
Tomorrow has come
But the sun died along with yesterday
I don't know what part of me I told
To settle down with the void.
A void brought on by the long night
Brought on by a fruit many thousands of years ago
Bit into by the eldest of us
To mark the separation
The falling away
Of us from the divine.
That deceptive serpent
The great dragon
That would see us all in Hell
But we won't go down without a fight.
The second Adam brought to us by God
A son
To bring us the missing light
That was stolen from us.
We are the elect
We will overcome the darkness
Though we have not understood the light
All will bow one day
When the Son returns
To eternally rule
When Gog and Magog are defeated
Then we will see the light.

100.

Light, my old friend
You've been gone for so long
Can I ever hope to see you again
When the world falls away
When my pain drains away?
I try to imagine the day
But it's been pulled from my memory
I try to imagine what causes the shadows
But I see no source, no hope
Just darkness
The long night
I once had the joy
That so many claim to have
But I found my own serenity
In a place far from home
A place to call my own
My Saviour has met me there
He comforts me in the gloom
To tell me, "Soon, child, soon."
But day can't come soon enough
I hear the preacher call for the judgement to come
But I yearn for the people to see the day
When the elect inherit the Earth
Though it seems like darkness is the victor
We hope for the coming light
When Yahweh has shown His face
And there are no longer the shadows
That I watch dancing on the wall
An entertaining story being told
Where all hope has been lost
But in my dark corner
I hope for the light
Though my tears may fall into a void
Created by my own doubts
The hope will come
The hope has come.

101.

I saw light
In the fire of candlelight
Soothing, comforting.
The shadows play games
Dancing behind me
The smell of burning wax
Attempts to calm me.
Do the demons in the dark
Hold bondage over me forever?
I know freedom lies in the light
Beholden.
Let Yahweh touch my lips
Cleanse the taint from me
With a burning coal
From righteous fire.
One day eternal light will come
But darkness must rule
Temporarily
The lawless one will rise
Before Christ ruled from Zion.
Where we will learn
From the holy throne.
For now, we wait
In the shadows
With a burning candle
To see hope.

102.

Glory shines
In the midst of
Darkness
That all may see the Lamb.
So many lies
Held under truth
When Judah's Lion
Takes His worthy throne.
The Earth itself awaits
For the arrival of her King
To give account of our
Stewardship.
The co-heirs will reign with Him
And be bathed in His love
No more pain
No more tears
As the soothing sound of
Falling rain
We will forever know Him
And meet Him at holy Zion.
To know truth
Intimately
Children of the most high
Warriors that no longer have to fight
We will forever be in tranquil
Peace.

103. Not Be Conquered

Modern world,
Old teaching.
It thinks it has discovered something new in these
Heresies,
But it has all been said before.
Falsehoods about Yahweh,
Disinformation of His bride,
It's nothing new
Nothing
Enlightened.
This falsehood has never destroyed us before,
Nor has when our blood flowed in the Roman arena,
Have we backed down from truth.
Yet the world attacks with old
Lies.
Thinking we can be conquered.
We can be beaten and murdered,
But never
Conquered.
Even the Elect may fall into the lie,
Becoming fares in a field of wheat,
But we will not be conquered,
Yahweh will uphold his
Truth.

104. Rising Hope

Never a winner
Don't want to be a sinner
All these dreams that leave me questioning
Can't break the callousness
But got to treat the fallenness
Disposing of winter
The ravenous splinter
Hope reborn in the spring awakening
Replant what's left of this
Raising up a prayerful fist
We can't remember
What made us Fall into this
Never again
The world is beautiful
Breathe in the colourful
Just can't be tempered
It causes us the cancer
In the night
The world is waiting now
It makes me smile somehow

105. Sparrows

Birds sing with the rising sun,
Morning sounds to usher in the new day,
The world aware of the fires of life,
With which we cannot hope to breathe
In the life we cherish.
Sparrows dig for worms,
Wriggling to gain a sense of
Freedom,
From gullets of young singers,
To fuel the mornings call.
The glory of the morning
Light we cherish,
From the very throne of Yahweh,
Whom we choose to forget,
The lamb,
The lion,
Of Judah.
Speaking day into existence,
The very power of his
Word.
A sound so sweet we often forget,
Hard to hear when life is so
Cluttered, with unimportant details.
Hope comes anew with the songs of
Birds and fires of the Son.
Though loving also
Judging.
Going throughout the world,
Bringing his Word to fruition,
Sustaining our being,
Reminding us,
With the songs of
Sparrows.

106. The Image

Defacing the face of Yahweh
By attacking the elect
Can we know Freedom?
Can the pain be relieved?

We are the image
Of the Holy One
Yet we suffer
Scarred and bruised
We try to get away from the Tormentor
Yet we're hunted
Like rabid dogs that are accursed

Yet we are the image
Salvation belongs to us
We bleed our blood
In soul-filled drops
There is no peace to be found here
Only the sword of war
Conflict follows us everywhere
Because the crowds do not understand

We are the image
We yearn for the New Jerusalem
Where these tears and the pain will cease
To be reunited with those we love
Who have been murdered
Killed for their beliefs, because

We are the image.

Ballads of Lost Lenoria: A Shadow's Cry Anthology

Introduction

So, this is a short collection of epic fantasy poetry. Given for mainly a table-top gaming audience but easily enjoyable by anyone. My passion for fantasy has been with me since I first read the greatest of fantasy epics in elementary and high school. There are elements of inspiration from all sorts of fantasy tropes, some will be easily recognizable, others you may need to do an internet search for to figure them out. And of course, there are biblical references as my faith would lead me to include these kinds of ideas in them.

I hope you enjoy this small volume. May it be the first of many to come!

- Anthony Uyl, President/Owner Devoted Publishing, Author

Lost Lenoria

A time long ago, forgotten to ages,
When rivers ran clear and blue,
The sea was treacherous,
The storms glorious and angry.
Yahweh spoke a world into being,
Formed from his will alone,
He created something pure and good,
Along with the hosts of heaven.
Spirits of ages past knelt to the lord of heaven,
But some rebelled and ruined this new world,
This new Lenoria, into corruption and despair.
They led races of men, elves, and dwarves,
To war against the gates of heaven.
Dragons raged the countryside,
Ancient demons burned the hearts of men,
Yet the ones that called on Yahweh's name,
Marched on the gates of Gehennorg,
To overthrow the rebellious king.
Blood was spilt, oaths were sworn,
Bound to an ancient gem, lost to time,
Was the lord of the demon host.
Though he raged against time,
For ages he has ruled,
Now bound to world he despised.
Peace reigned for a while,
But for how long?
Eventually the hearts of mortals gave way,
Evil found its root once more,
It is time for the righteous to stand firm,
To reclaim Lenoria once more.

The Elf Maid

And as the elven princess trod,
Along a road she had long forgot,
She dreamed of him, the forgotten king,
Of whom her dreams and songs did sing.

Her father bid her go aloft,
To lands long gone, away and soft,
Yet hard she chose the life to live,
Her very life to darkness give.

To face the shadow that has grown,
In the east that where haunts are known,
She'd rather face the growing night,
Even if it ever be her fright.

The king of man did forget her not,
Bearing her jewel with loyal fraught,
He dreamed of her but did not hope,
That united they'd be to forever cope.

She sent him love that he could not bear,
For he wished her to leave to realms so fair,
To be with her people to forget him so,
But her thoughts ever drifted to him not to go.

Though wars were fought, and legions lost,
She did care not about that cost,
Though blood was shed upon the cusp,
She knew he'd come just as he must.

For love so strong did she uphold,
Even if he convinced himself not told,
Yet she believed forever true,
That her elven blood ran right and blue.

The lady of light knew her heart,

That she could never him depart,
There was purity in her golden mind,
That no man will every truly find.
Though the fires of darkness spread,
She'll find her heart though when dead,
The flames of war do drain her heart,
That the man of life shall 'ere depart.

While hope may seem to all be lost,
There is no doubt to her the cost,
Though she doth die in pain of loss,
She dares not give in to the dirge and dross.

Where there be hope she doth believe,
That truth will ever come to conceive,
That he will return to her warm arms,
And sing to him her dearest songs.

Dark Rider Hunting

Hunting, searching, ever onwards,
For his masters forgotten glory,
The dark rider terrifying to behold,
Runs down the enemy to the fire.

An enemy anew threatens the land,
With determination to destroy,
The glory of the dark one,
A master that shall rule the land.

The dark rider gallops, upon a steed.
Given to them by someone they will betray,
But they know it not,
They pay their tribute to them, loyally.

But the glory of the fire, needs to be sated,
There it is traversing the land,
Once they were defeated by a king,
But not again, they will find the bearer, the great enemy.

Destruction is their name,
Ghosts of a forgotten age,
They rose at their masters' call,
Now they hunt forever for his beloved.

Only time will allow them to find,
The treacherous one of the new enemy,
That will inevitably be enslaved,
For his rebellion against their lord.

Gallop, dark rider,
Time is growing short,
The glory marches ever towards doom,
Time is short, the light is about to shine.

Dwarf King

Stalwart fighter, with a devoted heart,
The dwarf wields his axe so smart,
To cleave the orc and goblin alike,
Fighting ever onward, sharp as spikes.

The mountain hold cannot contain the grudge,
Towards the ones that betrayed the trudge,
When the fled their home from the fires wrath,
Only to return to halls torn from craft.

The warrior sits on a stone throne,
In the place once again his home,
After felling the invading tide,
To which he never tried to hide.

His brothers and kin hold his ear,
To give him tidings of things to bear,
The days are dark, evil has come,
It is not like them to go and run from.

The dwarven fighter cleaves to his will,
Just like gold that haunts him still,
To take vengeance on the realm of wood,
That hosts the evil that ever it could.

Spiders of old, and goblins of hate
Have tried to cower from him, but too late,
There is fire in his soul to reclaim the throes,
Of all that has been taken from him in rows.

Awaiting the Dawn

Wayward wanderer, traveling roads,
Forgotten and forlorn, in quiet country-sides,
Watching for evil tides, to sweep from the east,
Where the shadow grows, ever constant.

Creatures of darkness aroused by fright,
Broken by ancient vows sworn long ago,
To a dark lord that cares for nothing,
Nothing but himself and his will.

The wanderer travels on, watching the shadow,
Fighting the tide of grief that rolls ever on,
To make for hope that yet may die,
As long as he and his own do not fail in their duty.

Flowers of beauty that he fights for,
The dawning sun, ever warm,
To defend the wonderful world of old,
To await the dawn, and the joy it brings.

Hunt Some Orc

Run through the trees,
Evergreen and fragrant,
To chase the aberration,
The abomination,
That ruins the land,
Despoils the beauty of spring.
Avoiding the sunlight,
To bring the monster to bear,
Freeing captives,
Caught for food,
Blood pumps in our veins.
We must hurry,
The little ones won't last.
Heroes we are,
Set out to preserve,
The innocence of children,
By hunting some orc!

The Elven Queen

Fair and radiant,
The grass shines in her presence,
Gowns of pure daylight,
Draw around her.
To make her beauty emanate,
Hair of twilight,
Calls on the coming dawn,
That the sun will shine the fairer.
Light itself calls her name,
She commands the moon,
To rise in the night,
The sun to come at the time.
Sands of time can't hold her,
As she gleams in pure star light.
Immortal, beautiful,
Even dwarves pay her dues,
For nothing shall ever be called fairer,
Then the Elven Queen.

The Necromancer
Black robes filling the night
Breath of noxious vapors
Insects flee at the sight
Wolves come to the beckoned call.
Lords of death dance in the night
The dark one stands in solace
There is little life to be found
Where the lifeless one dawns.
He stretches out his hand
That eldritch energy may flow
Daylight crumbles at the call
As the ground begins to move.
A bone champion emerges
Free from the ever decay
Knowledge lost in twilight doom
To serve is to live.
A smile creeps forth
The warrior has come
What blasphemy will he taunt
As the necromancer calls his legion.

The Red Dragon
Iron scales concealing a cruel soul
Devouring innocent creatures.
He sits on a mountain of glittering
Gold.
Magic infuses the bones of the ancient wyrm
Damnation is his eternal calling.
Though nature be not his nurture
He gives in to the anger within
Of a mad world that pales his own
Sin.
The blasphemous name given him
By a wizard of long past due
There belongs no salvation to him.
Towns are razed and heroes consumed
All to his sadistic glee.
What divine and arcane power
Can liberate the world from his rage
Only the true power of Yeshua
Can bring him to his knees.
Until judgement comes there is little
Anyone can hope to attain
To fulfill his dark delights.
Where oh Lamb is your power?
The Lion that will curb his strength?
You will be subdued wyrm,
In slow and precious time!

Mountain Caretakers

Delving deep in mountains,
Gold that covets the hearts of men,
The dwarves rule with absolution,
Knowing that ever they will reign.
All desire the mountain,
Elves, humans, halflings,
Even the ancient dragons of old,
Yet none shall take these halls of stone,
From masters so wise and strong,
That the fortress is impregnable.
Many have tried, all have failed,
The fields of Achaiaer are stained in blood,
The blood of mortals and immortals alike,
The gods themselves may be powerless,
To strip the hall from the mountain king.
Ever was there mountains so tall,
A ridge of peaks that lined,
The spine of a world long forgotten,
Orcs used to rule here,
Now they are banished,
Relegated to realms of other weaker mortals.
They rule with surety,
Thinking they cannot be uprooted,
Yet evil arises,
Unlike anything seen before,
The king of lies has arisen,
A dark prince to come,
And demand his due,
Or watch these dwarves burn,
Burn in the inferno of eternity.

Giant Tyrants
A race of old,
Beyond the written word,
They arose from illicit marriages,
Born from the seed of angels and man.
The gods forbid it,
Yahweh himself condemned it,
Sending storms to punish the arrival,
Yet they survive.
Some walk dead,
Other rule in palaces of gold and crystal,
Yet their fury is still felt,
Enslaving nations to pay heed,
To a dark lord in the north,
That uses power of an unnatural sort.
Magic some call it,
Miracles others refer it,
Not right for mortal creatures is for certain,
Corrupting hearts and minds.
The lord of the fires,
Scourging the land and skies,
Comes for his own,
These kings and tyrants to form his kingdom,
And an army that will not be stopped.
Hundreds of thousands line their ranks,
Slaves and freemen alike march in black armour,
To enslave the world.
Who will rise to save the feeble,
And bring the age of peace,
Promised so long ago?

An Adventure

I sit here, peacefully,
No cares, no wonders, no desires,
Then I see you walk past,
Eyes so wonderous and I think,
What roads shall I travel?
What mountains shall I climb?
What forest shall I wander?
What rivers shall I swim?
To find the truest treasure,
Any man or elf could find,
To be enraptured by a maiden,
So elven, so divine.
I have no desire for gold,
Or treasures so bold and bright,
I once desired quiet,
The peace from the cool evening,
I promised myself I wound not,
Go out into the danger alone,
But there was something calling me,
That I had to leave my very home.
Break open my heart,
See what it is I would find,
To bring peace to my homeland,
Where no shadow will divide.
You bid me not go,
But it is evident to me,
That if I do not leave now,
I will never be at peace.

Forest for the Trees

The old world is passing away,
While the machine of industry comes,
Hopefully the old ways will not die,
As the wisdom it truly holds.
While the trees fall and ashen,
The elven lords do weep,
Their home is slowly fading,
And dreams fall ever so deep.
Though they war and string their bows,
The orc army marches onward,
To claim the precious forests,
For their dark lord in the north.
The slender and grace of the trees,
No other land can attest to,
Its majesty is unparalleled,
Nothing can compare to it.
Wisdom is held in those branches,
Wisdom of ages long gone,
If trees could speak, they would tell you,
Of when old races long gone, walked about.
The memories of old are slowly passing away,
As the dark forces hack and burn,
To make way for something new,
Something unwanted in this world.
Stand and fight for the forest's wisdom,
Elves march to war,
The queen of the trees will call you all,
To defend its beauty once more.

Evil Wizard

Scheming to rule men,
Not holding to his lofty place,
A tower built for evil,
While an army grows below him.
He writes his spells to conquer,
All the realms below him,
A servant of darker evils,
Though he does not know it.
The demons that speak to him in silence,
Tell him secrets long forgotten,
The lord of fire wants to devour him,
To take his power for his own.
The evil wizard plots destruction,
To grow power and greed,
He cares not at all for living things,
Just the necromantic arts, long lost.
Recruiting armies through treachery,
He walks about unseen,
Learning the secrets of mortal hearts,
So that he can offer lies unclean.
People fall to his sway,
His words sound true and just,
Yet filled with lies and malice,
There is nothing he will not promise.
He will not deliver on his word,
He means nothing true or pure,
By the time the slaves realize it,
They are already tainted beyond redemption.
Time to stand and fight for justice,
To rip his tower down,
Can the forces of light conjure,
Someone to ride to war and freedom?

Fortress of Heaven

Hewn of solid rock,
Standing tall over the rivers of old,
A fortress of men stands,
Stands to protect the mortal realms.
Wars have raged against this place,
To take down and feed of human blood,
But the craftsmanship of dwarves,
The cunning of elves,
Has never broken its gates down.
Many have tried,
Orcs, goblins, dark elves, hobgoblins,
All have tried to claim this place as their own.
None have succeeded,
Though the skill of men in battle,
Is limited compared to the ancient,
To the warlike races,
They have always held true to the protection,
The sturdiness of walls built long ago.
Graceful, yet strong.
Elegant, yet thick.
This fortress is a testament to things,
Of ancient alliances from millennia ago.
Many have tried to claim ownership over it,
Those that have long ago abandoned it,
For its halls and rooms are many and strong,
But the race of humanity has held it ever true.
They guard it as a royal sanctum,
Given to them by the gods themselves.
The darkness is coming though,
They must prepare,
For the gates of the Fortress of Heaven,
May not hold back this new, yet ancient, evil.

Orc Lord

Where he comes from, no one knows,
He has fought in wars uncounted,
Bled more mortals than can be numbered,
All fear his name when it passes their tongues.
Baladan, the black orc of Beelzebub,
First of his master's servants.
He fights for not reason,
Other than to feast on human flesh,
Once, he too, was a human,
But his dark master made him corrupt,
And perfect for evil.
Although time should have claimed his soul,
Immortal he has become,
Many have thought to have slain him dead,
Yet time and time again,
He rides new hordes to war.
Never will he find peace,
Until the world is covered in flame,
At his master's command.
He desires nothing than to carve new flesh,
To break the souls of all,
To make them bow before him,
And be enslaved to the will of the dark father.
He cares not for gold, or jewels,
Just blood of flesh.
For conquering.
The storm is coming when orcs will come,
With Baladan at their head,
Heroes will need to rise up,
If he is to be taken down,
For the world to have hope once more.

Elven Lord

Regal, majestic,
He rides on a white horse,
Bred for war,
To free the mortal realms from despair.
His blades dance in battle,
While the enemy cannot approach,
Without feeling the touch of steel,
The cold release of life.
Many years of training,
Have given him glorious skill,
Even in arts of kingship,
To rule with justice and might.
None question his wisdom,
He has tried the greatest and best,
His learning is beyond compare,
Even the ancient wizards do not equal.
When the world comes to the brink of war,
He will respond with cunning,
Though prideful that he cannot be beat,
The wars of the evil one will come.
His queen rules by his side,
As just and wonderful as he,
She keeps him upright and true,
So that all may love both of them.
He does not stand alone,
Only by the grace of their heavenly lords,
He has seen the gates of heaven,
In holy and prophetic dreams.

Dead Armies

Many do not think it possible,
For the dead to walk the realms,
But there is power,
Dark power,
Capable or raising the dead from their tombs.
In these dark and evil days,
The skeletons and zombies walk,
Destroying the living that walk at night,
Even the innocent, the fragile.
They care not for gold,
Only wanting to see pestilence,
Cover the face of the earth.
Where they go, disease easily follows,
Since these armies do not care,
About anything under the sun.
Debasing living flesh,
To raise new soldiers,
Men, women, children, all,
They kill without thought,
Without mercy.
The living are of no use to them,
All must die and suffer their wrath,
To be raised again in the dusk,
So they can carry on the war.
A dark lord from the north gives them their power,
None can stand before them,
All will fall,
All will fade.

The Mountain Pass

Danger lurks on every peak,
But the mountains must be crossed.
A spine of peaks that stretch,
Across the world and back,
Hiding secrets and realms,
Long forgotten, long lost.
Creatures of evil roam the paths,
Preying on those that they would encounter,
To feed their dark wills,
And weaken frail hearts.
Brave men wander these stretches,
To rid the passes of such filth,
But they always come back,
They always hunt.
Heroes have been lost,
Legends never found,
From the creatures lurking here.
The bravest of souls are the ones,
Who comes here for a simple trek.
To come here unprepared,
Will be a journey most dire,
For if you do not worry yourself,
With what is behind the next cleft,
What waits there may take your soul.

The Drow Princess

In caverns below the earth,
Deep in forgotten realms,
Where the sun never touches the rock,
And light never brings new life.
Cities are kept and breathe,
Life is bustling, but sad.
Mighty warriors, hidden from the light,
With skin black as night,
Hair white as the stars,
But cruel as vipers,
Pitiless as the dragons they keep.
Worshipping dark gods best forgotten,
A princess arises.
Something is different in her,
This dark elf, filled with hope and light,
Breaks free from her royal family,
That oppress all that come under their reign,
To flee to the surface, where again she is in chains.
Crowds want to hang her,
For the crimes of her race,
One man, a human,
Should be opposed to all she is,
But shows her grace, shows her love.
Many despise them for their charity,
She fights to show a new way to her oppressors,
For she was not born evil,
Like so many assume,
But born of goodness amongst the dark.

White Wolf

East of the great mountains,
The great spine of the world,
A creature dwells,
Horrible and ferocious.
Many mistake him for a wolf,
But he is larger, stronger,
Able to rip and tear with little effort.
Woodsmen have hunted him,
To bring his pelt for a bounty,
But he cannot be stopped,
He is the white wolf of Aragband.
Once he was a man,
Noble and arrogant,
Who ruled lands ancient and rich.
Until a gypsy cursed him,
Transformed him to this,
So that he would learn humility,
And be restored to his glory.
Time has forgotten him,
The sun has set on his due,
His humility grew to frustration,
Frustration to anger,
Anger to madness.
He remembers not who he was,
Or what he has to gain,
Just the anger of being forgotten,
Of being hunted by those once his own.

Southern Jungles

Deep to the south of the lands of humans,
Where even the ancient elves refuse to go,
Lay jungles of ancient horrors,
Lying in wait for anyone to enter their home.
These are reptiles, lizards,
That walk like men, but are twice their size.
They even talk and reason,
Build and fashion,
Yet most consider them beasts.
They fear the world outside the jungle,
Outside of the heat they find comfort in.
The gold and jewels they make into weapons,
Realizing not the worth of their crafts,
If they only knew the wealth that lay within their cities,
They would be lords of the world,
Mightier than even the dwarf kings.
But they have been punished,
Exiled,
For what they are,
Nobody thinks them as people.
Their hatred knows no bounds,
For the slaves they have been made into,
At the hands of poachers,
That see them as nothing more than animals.
Fight brave lizardmen,
Fight and prove your worth.
The world needs new warriors,
New blood,
To fight the coming ancient terrors.

Temple Lords

Men-like bulls guard the ancient temples,
Built long ago by forgotten hands.
Even the elves in all their elegance,
Look at wonder at these halls.
The Minotaurs do not allow them access,
Secrets within are theirs.
Too many have tried to pry their way in,
But these mighty warriors send them back.
Horrible they are to behold,
Tall and proud with great axes in hand.
These warriors are strong,
Years spent in combat make them equals,
To the greatest warriors of the orc and elven halls.
Yet they are few.
These ancient temples are falling one by one,
As the ancient darkness returns.
These halls to Yahweh are being defiled,
In an attempt to subdue his strength.
The Minotaurs fight back this storm,
They will not yield to the night.
Truth is their armour,
Light is their axes,
Yet the night continues to press on.
Many of their number have folded to the infernal,
Many of their brothers have the nobles had to kill.
This civil war will ensue until one is defeated,
Until the darkness overcomes,
Or the light is able to stand firm.

The Paladin
Noble warrior, imbued with the power of Yahweh,
To dispatch the undead and infernal.
He wanders the world,
Fighting for the light,
Fighting for honour,
For an order of knights that may no longer exist.
His morningstar flashes in the night,
As he breaks the oncoming hordes,
To free the innocent,
The meek,
And make them free from tyranny.
He weeps over the state of the world,
He knows a darkness has returned,
To fight it back is his desire,
How this will happen, he does not know.
His duty is simple,
To defend all,
Whether humble or proud,
Even good or evil,
If they are innocent,
He is called to defend.
But he walks the road alone.
No one will join him,
His sanctimonious mission is too much for them.
Greed has no place in his heart,
Nor arrogance.
He fights for righteousness,
Hoping one day, he will find peace in this dark place.

Knights of Sanctity

Riding in file,
In a holy march,
A quest to reclaim the land.
Taken by orcs and demon kin,
The knights ride on.
Gallant horses and mighty men,
Wear armour of polished steel,
Gleaming white in the sunlit hours,
Shining dutifully in the pale moonlight.
Their holy call drives them forth,
Vows of purity not taken lightly,
Ever marching onward to battle,
To purify land and kingdom.
Each anticipates the coming death,
With fearless honour they push forth.
To die is gain,
The eternal peace,
Brought on by promises of the divine.
Sworn to oaths in holy temples,
This order of knights hates all defilers,
Of places of holiness and purity.
The orcs dare not stand against them,
These knights' numbers are too great.
Still the orcs line up for war,
Hoping their ferocity will win out in the end.
These warriors fear not death or pain,
So bravely they charge the fold.
Though the orcish tribes inhabit the fortress,
Captured by nobles of the land,
The knights charge forward,
Lances down,
Shields of faith borne with hope.

Wrath of War

The world is changing,
What was once peaceful and true,
Is now corrupt and debased.
The rumours of war are spreading,
Lenoria is on the brink of destruction,
Too many foes are arising,
Foes of old and ancient terror.
Demons have sprung from the deep,
Balors, fiends of the pit and more.
Guardians of ancient wonder,
Have tried to arise to counter them,
But the lords of heaven have left it,
Left it in the hands of mortals.
The elves, dwarves and humans must unite,
Or else they all will fall.
Too many of these peoples have too much anger,
Too much hatred for ancient grudges,
Uniting will not be an easy task.
Guides are sent,
Knights of holy orders,
To try and correct the old prejudices,
Yet this may not be enough.
The march of the orcs and dead has begun,
Drumbeats are heard on the wind,
To the distant ears of the north and south,
And the east and west.
Fright is filling all peoples' hearts,
Ancient powers may have to come,
To save the children of the heavens,
There is too much to do,
Too much to do before the war comes,
Before the innocent start to perish,
And all that is left,
Is memory.

Purifying Fire

A wizards' wrath descends on the foes,
Scorching flesh and bone,
To weaken their wills,
And blacken their twisted souls.
The fire purifies the stench within,
Removing the taint from this unholiness.
The foes attempt to take the tower,
To claim the power as their own.
The fire continues raining from heaven,
Consuming grass and trees,
So that the great enemy may not advance.
The wizard knows time is short,
His power will not last forever,
So, he prays to heaven for reprieve,
To be taken away to serve another day.
Magic has its limit,
When power is not fulfilled.
The fire while doing its mighty work,
Will diminish,
It will fail.
The purifying power will cease,
The corruption will grow again,
A plague inserting itself,
Into the hearts of all around.
Disease it is to feeble minds,
Disrupting created flesh,
To something only the lords of hell can admire.
The fire must continue,
As long as it must, it must continue.
Or all will feel the wrath,
All will fall.

The Ancient River

A mighty river old and pure,
Flows from a single source,
That no one has been able to find.
Many have tried to follow it,
Yet it goes onward,
Onward,
Never to end.
It is rumoured to originate,
In the gardens of Lenoria,
Where the first elves, dwarves and humans were born.
When all people were united under one banner,
Under one truth.
Many have tried to find the garden,
Seeking the river as it cleanses the land.
Its waters are pure and healing,
Seeping with power of the divine.
Many make pilgrimages to these waters,
To heal the plagues and diseases of the flesh,
And the detriments of the soul.
Some see the river itself as divine,
Yet it is no god,
Just has the power of the divine within it.
The elves themselves drew their immortality from it,
The dwarves their keen stonework,
Humans drew their passions.
Other races have tried to corrupt the river,
But it has resisted all attempts.
No dark power has been able to destroy,
The divine power of this river,
A river with no name,
But filled with life.

The Great Sea

Chaotic with storms,
Storms that sink the mightiest galleons,
Ravage the surface of the deep.
The lords of heaven themselves,
Use the sea as a barrier to guard against,
Innocent lands beyond.
Where corruption and greed have yet to reach,
Where orcs and dead have yet to war.
Leviathan and Rahab guard the depths,
Sinking the ships that dare the breadth,
No one has been able to pass,
Without contending with these dragons,
Dragons of the mighty sea.
All races have tried to pass,
Believing there are riches abounding,
On shores of pure sunlight.
Yet no one has seen,
No one has the skill to cross the waves,
That crash on shores and hulls.
The rocks that jut out from suspicious spots,
To ground the ships in the midst of the sea.
Mighty divine power guards the depths,
Where ships and creatures of old find their rest.
Some quest in the sea to hunt the creatures,
Creatures of myth and lore,
To claim a trophy unlike any other.
But the sea will claim them all,
The monsters will emerge and take them down,
Before they can even blink an eye,
Or breathe a cry for help.

Charron's Herald

Some sit in the quiet night,
Before a great battle to come,
Watching the lakes and rivers,
For a herald, a harbinger of doom.
They say when a skiff,
Carrying a single poleman,
Dressed in long robes,
And a skulled head,
Comes up to the shore,
That death has come to them all.
A herald of doom,
Of eternal torment,
To carry souls to the realms of Sheol,
There to be held until the return of majesty.
Some think him a demon,
A servant of dark and angry lords,
But no one knows for sure,
All fear the sight, if and when he comes,
While others pray for hopes that he will not arrive.
If he comes, wars are called off,
Peace is attempted,
So that damnation will not fall.
Everyone fears the boatman,
No one willing to pay his price,
To cross the Styx and see the dead lands,
To see the realms where only some may rest.
Too many fear the pit,
That awaits them in Sheol,
Still others fear the unknown,
That arrives with the Herald of Charron.

Glade of the Druids

Hidden deep in the Elvenwood,
Where trees have long grown,
To hide the realms of natures guardians,
Who prefer to remain hidden,
Secluded.
There is an open glade,
Beautiful it is, filled with heaven's light,
Reaching through the trees,
To streams with shores of flowers,
And cleansing water of starlight.
Ancient wonders are found here,
Buried deep within the soil,
Powers forgotten since long ago.
That the druids quietly protect.
They know the power of the Elvenwood,
Even if the elves who live here do not.
The trees have knowledge unfounded,
Forgotten long ago by all peoples.
The druids fear the evil to come,
That it may reach the glade.
They have prepared for war,
To protect this ancient glade,
So that darkness may not overpower it.
Ancient treemen have answered the call,
Of the ancient archdruid,
To protect what they hold most dear,
The power of nature itself.
This glade is the epicentre of nature's glory,
Some believe to be the Garden of Lenoria itself,
If it is true, the druids are not saying,
But evil is eager to find out,
So that it can set up a throne in the ancient glade.

Nymph Queen

A guardian of the wood and lakes,
This most beautiful creature,
Takes and makes a home.
She is sworn to defend her lands,
Against all perversion of mortal flesh,
With a beauty that enraptures,
Even the strongest of will.
Those that fail to resist her,
Are not able to break the power of her will,
As she commands them as simpletons,
In all aspects of her power.
The realms she lives in,
Is also a home of the elves,
The forest of Symgate,
An alliance to defend it from the outside world.
She is sworn to marry the elven king,
As a symbol of this alliance,
Though they are not able to have offspring,
The marriage is symbolic,
So that all may see the power in their union.
The queen rules her own as her own,
With no influence from others,
Defending the deepest of the woods,
Where ancient powers dwell,
Forgotten, unwanted.
Her allies, apart from the elves, are many,
As she is able to seduce even the strongest man.
Spies all over the world she has put in place,
Making her the most knowledgeable creature alive.
If any would want to know,
The deepest secrets of the world,
They should seek her out.
But beware her beauty,
Or your quest for knowledge will be over,
As you become her most willing slave.

Tower of Night

Deep in the wastes of the east,
Where sand and stone rule the land,
And the dead are present in the long-lasting night.
A tower has been raised,
To signal the rulership of a dark lord,
A lord who neither sleeps nor rests,
But rules with cruelty and malice.
He feasts on the souls of mortals,
Rejoices in the nightmares of children,
And ravages the armies of all.
The orcs and the dead serve him,
They march as one under a banner of doom,
To sound his siren song in the depths,
Of a world that wants to forget him.
Too many have tried to write him off,
As myth, as legend, best left to imagination.
Yet the armies march once more,
The wisemen of the white towers of humans,
And the crystal towers of elves,
Have all foreseen his coming.
Many have ruled from this tower in ages past,
But none have exerted the will of madness,
Madness and malice this lord empowers.
This will sends the armies forward,
With power and cunning unlike any before.
What hope is there that the tower will fall,
With its lord into a pile of rubble?
The stonework is ancient, forgotten by even dwarves,
The workmanship exquisite,
Yet it is evil,
Shall goodness prevail,
When such darkness is present,
In a world that prefers ignorance?

Temptations of Gold

Dwarves hide in their golden halls,
Hoarding the gold they acquire.
Riches so deep and wonderful,
Yet they share it with no one.
They could finance nations and armies,
To be the best they could be,
With gleaming armour,
And razor-sharp swords,
Yet they keep it for themselves,
To make their treasuries vast beyond measure.
Their skills are deep and wonderful,
The most precious monuments,
Of gold and other metals,
Stand tall in their halls.
The yellow shimmer glows in their mountains,
In their kingdoms of stone,
The gold shimmers and shines.
Their hearts are filled with greed,
And the armies of darkness would take it all.
If the dwarves do not seek forgiveness,
For their greed and arrogance,
Then judgment will fall on them.
Their halls are strong and well armed,
Due to the gold their hoard,
But the armies of evil are greater,
Can their gold save them from death?
They cannot take it with them,
There is no place for riches in the death lands,
Yet they try to make themselves wealthier,
Richer in state,
To what end?
What will all these temptations lead to,
If not their utter ruin?

The Guild
Quiet and secretive,
Everyone knows they are there,
But no one knows who is a member.
Like shadows on the walls,
They watch without ceasing,
Biding their time of when to strike,
When to steal,
When to kill.
The fear of their wrath,
Fills the poor and disadvantaged,
As they are the slaves to their will,
The will of the guild's lords.
They take from those that have not,
To make themselves richer,
Though they need not the wealth,
Like all greed they desire more.
Power is also a craving,
Mayors and kings have paid them due,
Giving them work to undue political foes,
To keep their hands clean,
And make themselves seem benevolent,
When indeed they are not.
The guilds have their secrets,
They could tear kingdoms down,
But they do not want a public face,
But to remain hidden, unseen,
Awaiting a time once more,
To steal or kill.

Robed Pilgrim
A mysterious wanderer,
No one knows his name,
Or where he comes from.
Fighting for justice,
Quietly undoing the powers of evil.
Some see him as a prophet,
A return of an ancient priesthood,
A mediator between mortals and heaven.
He does not speak of his mission,
Just visits the lowly places,
Fighting the darkness in the home.
Believing that goodness has to start,
In the heart before the kingdom.
Sure, he believes evil must be fought,
But evil must not take hold,
In the hearts and minds of all people.
He speaks truth and morality,
To all who will listen,
And brings the sword down on those who oppose,
Those who would keep the people,
The innocent, in bondage.
He bears power from heaven,
To accomplish his task.
Many fear his coming,
Knowing they may be a target.
He loathes the darkness,
Persists against it,
Yet shows mercy and justice,
To everyone willing to repent.

Tavern Tales

In every city and town,
The tavern awaits all,
All who would come,
To find work or drink,
Song and dance,
Food and comfort.
Travellers from far and wide,
Find their way to this place,
To speak of their adventures,
To build fame and fortune,
Or to forget the horrors,
Horrors of a coming darkness.
Most are mercenaries,
Swords for hire,
Others are spies, seeking discontent,
In the best place known.
Still others wait for a time,
To rise up and be heroes,
To bring the light of heaven,
In a realm falling to night.
The greatest of heroes are found here,
As they are the brave,
The willing and foolish,
To face any fear,
Any monster,
For those willing to award them coin,
Coin that is much desired for their schemes.
All wait for the right heroes to come,
To find their fill of drink and food,
So that the evils ever present in the world,
Can be fought and subdued.

Forgotten Places

There are places in Lenoria,
Forgotten and alone.
Places of power,
Places of peace,
Where some have seen the passage of time,
And others have slept awaiting their epoch.
In some places elder things await,
Some evil,
Some benevolent,
Yet all await the coming war.
Other places are sullen and forlorn.
No one remembers them,
Though they are important,
To the success of heaven or hell,
But they will be discovered again.
Towers, forests, mountains, valleys,
All have a part to play,
Even if no one is there to guard them.
All will answer the call in the time to come,
The time of the destiny of good or evil.
No one can know what role they will play,
No one can know,
For they have forgotten,
Forgotten the importance of these unknown,
Peaceful and sometimes dark realms.
The war will hinge on the capture,
The conquering of realms of glory.

Bard's Song

Here comes now the end of the tales,
Of stories old and enemies new,
To those who would listen,
To the songs sung about these times.
Heroes are needed,
Now more than ever.
Armies must soon march,
To fight the darkness,
To combat the slavery to come.
We take for granted,
The freedom we have,
To be heroes everyday,
In the battle for the light.
Songs anew will always be sung,
To warm the hearts of children,
To warm the hearts of warriors,
So that they will rise up and fight,
Since so many want to hide,
Hide away and do nothing.
Cast not your fears away,
For they will give you strength,
To realize what must be fought,
What must be conquered.
Listen to the tales in all the towns,
To learn of what evils to confront,
Get your strength from the cares,
The cares of the people you love.
For they will carry you through,
So that you will have your own song,
Your own song and ballad,
To sing to the next generation.

A Shadow's Cry: The Song of the Vampire

Introduction

What to say in an introduction of a poetry book about vampires? First off, the term "vampire" isn't used in the poetry rather the term "shades" instead. This is because while vampires are definitely unbiblical, I've tried to give a biblical perspective about vampires and their origins. A group of ancient peoples from the Middle East, known as Rephaim, were a group of people whose Hebrew name translates into "shade." Ironically, this is also the name of the souls in the Hebrew underworld.

Let's be clear, the historical Rephaim and shades were not the same people. The historical people were not undead or returned spirits, but rather just a group of people that for some reason were associated with the same name. This poetry book takes some artistic license in attributing the two together. This in no way makes any truth claims as this is a piece of epic fictional poetry.

So, I invite you to enjoy the reading. New myths, some old stories will be told as a vampire, or Shade, tries to wrestle with the beauty that is mortality, and the love of a person that he has encountered unlike any he has encountered before.

- Anthony Uyl, President/Owner Devoted Publishing and Author

Dead and Sunshine

Something calls inside my aching soul,
To touch a fire that would consume me,
But the sight of that one makes me think,
That even this dead one can be made alive.
Though the years have not been kind to me,
I see an innocence so filled with grace,
My blood spurs me onwards, for one moment,
One taste, of innocence, that I've lost.
Never since I died in Enoch's womb,
Have I felt my heartbeat once more,
Though I walked the fields of Sheol,
And judged the kings that came down to me,
I yearn for the touch of fire once more.
That sunlight may consume my soul,
But is it worth it, for one human moment?
Living minds have no idea what they have,
What their innocence does to the ancient ones,
That have bled, that are dead,
That no longer feel with the hearts of men.
I know the dream is far off,
Life can never fill these veins again,
Hope is something I have lost so long ago,
Yet that sunshine shines and I hope,
Though it may rip me apart,
I hope.

Skin and Dreams

The darkness it folds around me,
My blood runs cold, like ice,
There is no heart that can behold me,
What has this death brought?
Your bullets cannot phase me,
Iron skin, organs of steel,
The blades of old are rusted,
When my flesh is wrought by them.
I see the cross that frees me,
I know it loves me still,
It has not forsaken my dead soul,
To bring me fire once again.
Is there redemption for one as myself?
Did I not slay the innocent for sport,
And make the childless my slaves?
If a blade could hurt me, I would dream.
Even dreams evade me,
Only nightmares enter my sleep,
To haunt me in the nights I wake,
Tormenting me with the future I await.

Dead Desires

Why don't people simply understand,
How beautiful it is to be, human?
The gentle pull of the breeze in your hair,
As you breathe in the smell of the flowers.
There are those dark ones,
Those lost souls,
That feel not the wind or smell the roses,
We have lost so much and gained so little.
Do you really want to be super-human?
To be dead like us and unable to feel?
I've tried to justify my existence,
To see the death as a gift.
I've been able to bend the will of men,
To consume the heart of the strong,
And con the smartest of minds,
But nothing compares with the meekness,
The gentleness of a living heart.
I have become awkward,
Unable to relate to the greater world,
No one wants to look in the shadows,
To understand how it doesn't breathe,
Doesn't feel,
Just lives in deathless agony,
For the things of humanity, of beauty.

Forever Lost

I dream in silence,
Of when I touched your skin,
And fed on your life,
Drank in your breath.
I tried to make you see,
To make you believe,
Yet you wanted it,
I craved the moment,
The instance,
Of the death.
I desired to see the blood,
The last drop of life,
To enter my veins,
Yet for all my craving,
I still felt love.
There was still need,
To see life in your eyes,
That light,
That hope of all things.
What you made me believe,
Cannot be explained,
Cannot be explored.
Yet you died in my arms,
Forever losing part of myself.

Memories

Memories,
They can haunt me,
When I see the light in your eyes.
It makes me crave the touch,
Of a life I once knew,
To remember the embrace,
Of something I have forgotten.
Your face is an echo,
Of something I once had,
Before the darkness came,
And took away my soul.
The life I felt then,
Boils the blood in me now,
As I try to smell the fragrance,
Of a spring I never knew.
I cannot be angry,
At the sweetest memory,
Brought on by your lips,
Though it aches me in the core,
The core of a housed beast.
Though I want to rage out,
And watch the world drown,
The memory of something lost,
Holds me back,
Makes me dream again,
Memories.

The Beast in Me

The beast calls to me,
To ruin and dreams,
To intake your life,
Leave you distraught and afraid.
The urge is undeniable,
Like red rage overtaking me,
This death I have as my own,
Comes with this ticket I cannot pay.
Flee from me,
Oh, innocent one!
There is no safety to be found in my wake,
I am the death you do not seek.
I crave the thing you fear,
To see the fear in your eyes,
And the pulse of your beating heart,
The beast longs for it, the hunt.
I try to supress it,
To revel in your mortal beauty,
Ponder your fleshly innocence,
Yet the roars in my head consume me.
The beast will not be tamed,
One day it will lash out,
Can your warmth subdue the fury?
And bring peace to my troubled mind?

The Prey

You were only the hunted,
I preyed and sought redemption,
But your blood called out,
To join me in the eternal night.
I wanted the taste of iron wine,
To fill my senses,
Quiet the monster within me,
Silence your breath in one twist.
Yet the covenant called to me,
To preserve life for my own,
So that I could live eternal,
And prey for you once more.
How funny it turned out,
Who the prey really was,
The radiance of your mortality,
Made my monsters hunger subside.
While you cut your skin to feed my lusts,
Offered your flesh to my hunger,
I couldn't take it away from you,
I needed to preserve you, your purity.
While I know I will be hunted for this,
For showing compassion,
Something not in my nightly nature,
I couldn't take it away, as prey.

Death Penalty

They saw me, the Elders,
The chance of them using you against me,
Most probably,
I am wanted dead, truly dead,
For believing, in life.
Believing that you could save me.
I am old you see,
A son of the one Enoch,
They have tried to control me,
My children,
My sons,
My daughters,
Born of my blood,
Brought back from the lands of Sheol.
They want to make me pay,
For seeing the beauty in mortals,
Believing that God himself could forgive.
They are demons, monsters
Greater monsters than me,
They just want to feed,
While I,
I want to hope.

Damnation

I fell away to the depths of Earth,
To cry in pits of tar and fire,
Crying tears of blood in agony,
For my cold heart which cannot feel.
Pitched against the realm of modern man,
To make me dead and not understand,
There is no fire to quench my soul,
Rising in a flood of tears for the old.
Your touch made me rethink the ways,
The pains that consumed my mind,
To take me away from this hell,
From the tortures in Sheol where I dwelt.
The bondage from the moment of birth,
To this state of death may not be freed.
As hard as you try to look in my eyes,
To assure me that there is something inside.
Stabbed, burned, broken, and scorned,
What can anyone know of my pains?
When I died too many eons ago,
To be born again after the trials of the hells.
Not sure I can be called human,
After the things I've felt and done,
To relinquish the pain of seeming eternity,
Do you not think I am worth the time?
To be born in a new death is special,
But not in the way that you perceive,
I am the damned one, sent here to reap,
Why would you dare to touch me, and cry?

Truth and Darkness

What did you see,
When I first gazed in your eyes?
Was it damnation, or salvation?
Did the fear of eternity take hold,
Or did the desire for the ages,
Creep into your fragile soul?
I have tried to show you,
To show you the true light,
Borne upon a cross so long ago,
But you wanted to touch my darkness,
The death I carry with me.
Was there fire in that cold depth?
Or an icy tomb filled with pain?
The truth is not what I wanted for you,
To see me in this damnation,
To save you from this death,
Yet you wanted to join,
Not to be in forever with this.
Could I live the rest of forever without you?
Did the blood I inherited before time,
Predict the coming of your light?
I tried to show you,
Yet you showed me so much more.

Take My Life

Did you come here to take my life?
Or did I come to you to finally die?
For these eras of time, I have desired,
To be laid in peace with the tombs of my fathers.
No one has known just how to put me down,
Even the eldest of my kind struggle,
To find a way to silence me,
For the heresy of protecting a mortal one.
Yet, for some reason you have resisted,
The yearning I can put in anyone's heart,
To die once and rise again,
You continue on, wanting to live.
You know you will one day die,
And I cannot bear the thought of this world.
A big, cold world without the light of you,
And it brings me down to a grave,
A grave that will not accept me.
I have slept to long to drown away,
The nightmares that plague me each day,
The waking screams that haunt me,
All day I think of you without me.
Eternity has never been so long,
To endure since the day you came along,
Made me feel the fire of mortality once more,
The beauty of fragility, that marks your grace.

Red Thirst

There is a hunger inside,
You cannot possibly understand,
When I smell you on the wind,
It makes my heartbeat with fury.
I have tried to satiate my appetite,
With a blood other than that of mortals,
But it always returns,
More ravish and demanding than ever.
You cannot see how I must walk,
In a world of blood and flesh,
That makes me want to drink,
From a cup I cannot give back.
I am old, older than the sands,
While one time I hungered and fed,
I have seen the light of the anointed,
When he hung on the tree and forgave me.
I did not deserve it, mortals received it,
Yet, I was given the chance at redemption,
Though I see the frailty in your skin,
The sin of blood still pulls at me.
Is there freedom from this pain,
To make me able to touch once more?
In order to feel the warmth of the son,
And live once again, reborn?

History is a Lie

We have always been here,
Hunting, destroying,
While you flounder through the streets,
In drunken forays of pleasure.
We are the darkness,
That will never come to light,
Needing to hide to survive,
Though we are strong, we are few.
If the world knew of the war,
Between us and the living,
We would be overrun and killed,
Forever, never to rise again.
Is it time for us to come out?
So many false prophets have arisen,
To pull away from the one truth,
Could we speak our filth,
And show ourselves to the world,
To not fear being hunted,
By the holy orders,
By the inquisitions,
By our own descendants?
That time may come, when we can hold hands,
In the twilight while we sleep,
To not fear being hunted and killed again,
By hands craving what we have,
And refuse the gift to them.

Your Fragrance

Your fragrance, pulls at my soul,
Not the perfume,
Not the flowers you shower yourself in,
But your flesh, your blood.
It is wine to my tongue,
Sweetness like honey in my gut,
I can smell it above all else,
Above the toxic showers of fragrance, that you try to hide in.
The predator in me,
Hungers for your life, your innocence,
The beast makes me strive to detect that scent,
And make your life mine.
I cannot control it at times,
Though you have shown me anew,
Something I have not known,
My nature compels me to feed.
I know there is no forgiveness,
My appetite is uncontrolled,
My sin is open for all to see,
What redemption to mortals is there within me?
Too many smells,
Like a dog towards fresh meat,
I crave the taste of blood,
Your fragrance compels me to come.
You may try to hide,
My preternatural senses are too strong,
Heightened by the age within me,
You smell, like fire.

A Calling

I reach out with my mind,
To call all like me to myself,
To prepare for judgment,
They think I do not know, but I do.
All their sins and slaughters,
I have seen in my own mind,
Though I have done worse,
So much worse, I stand as their judge.
The time of the undead must end,
New light, new hope speaks it so,
I have called down the powers of the end,
To bring mortals to the fold.
Do you not realize that all must one day end?
The creator himself can only sustain,
The undead race must move on,
Allow mortal flesh its time in space.
There are those that will resist,
A war is sure to ensue,
Though I can call them, each by name,
I cannot control them.
The mortal realms will know nothing like it,
The blood, the feuds, all must be answered,
Clans of elders will call me to account,
As well, I must answer my own call.

Power of Will

Why do you want to know,
How I move like the wind,
Fly through the stars,
Or move through the mists of time?
How I turn into a wolf,
A harbinger of evil,
The black plague of desire,
Or else make time stand still?
You think it magic, or devilry,
But it is more simple than that,
I desire, I do,
I will, it happens,
It is nothing more than moving a muscle,
Flexing an arm,
Twitching a leg.
It is natural for me to overpower a mortal,
And take his life blood from him.
I have no ability beyond my curse,
Humans desire to have my gifts,
Without the curse that comes with it.
Could you live without the sun,
For the rest of your immortal lives?
Could you stand to be cold, ever cold,
Never to feel the warmth?
Yes, there is giftings,
But curse, oh the curse,
Has driven the sanest man,
To babble,
In utter madness.

Shall I Create

You want to live forever,
I do not think you know what you ask,
The eternal torment of immortality,
It is not the gift you think it is.
Shall I feed you my blood,
While you die in my arms?
True you will not have to taste death,
But the never-ending night,
Consumes even the best of us.
I can bring you to the brink of death,
I can drip my unlife into your veins,
Yet I do not think this is what you want.
Shall the beauty of your mortality,
Be stripped from your flesh?
It is difficult to imagine the curse,
That cannot be ever reversed.
The heavenly father never promised us life,
Never guaranteed this curse would end.
This is not what you want.
When I beheld your beauty,
When your eyes fell on me,
I knew you would ask me for this,
But I cannot,
I shall not.
You need to live your life,
I need you to live.

Unchangeable

We are stuck,
In a state of ever trepidation.
We do not live,
Or learn,
There is no desire,
No passion,
Just stone, cold and solid.
We have never tried to be better,
Be new or updated.
There simply is no desire to be.
We are stuck in our ways,
As worlds come and go,
We remain the same.
I mourn over the days of old,
When the father of heaven,
Still walked amongst men.
Will that day come again,
When the glory of him,
Will slay us all?
And we cannot be saved,
Because we will not adapt,
Or change into who we were meant to be.
Is there something more,
That I cannot comprehend?
If we are able to be changed,
To grow,
Into something new,
Will it be beautiful?
Will it be as you?
I cannot fathom,
What I would become,
If I was able to become, something.

The Craving

I see you,
Dancing to the music,
The spheres shining their ancient light,
There are others around you,
Seeing your grace,
Wondering what you have.
Although I know what you desire,
Your own should give you something,
Something I cannot give.
You deserve a love,
A pure mortality,
I cannot love you the way you want,
Why should you continue to come to me,
Is what I have really so alluring?
Is death really what you want?
I want you have something more,
My cold flesh is not enough.
Some day I wish you were not here,
My heart would bear the weight easier,
To the eternal life I must live.
I do not want you to live with the curse,
But I want you to be able to love,
As a person loves,
To have a family,
Grow old and know paradise.
A paradise I will never know,
For when I finally am destroyed,
All I will see again,
Is Sheol.

Evil

I am born of evil,
A thing that should not be,
Others I have sired,
I have created,
To be just as evil,
Depraved.
Though I hunt them,
To try and extinguish their dark flame,
Evil will always be here,
Because it bears my name.
I do not know what hope remains,
Whether others will arise,
Forgiveness is so far gone for me,
Yet, I will try to make amends.
I owe the world ages of regret,
For what I done to it,
Humanity does not even know who I am,
Yet I try to redeem it all.
There is something more to all of this,
I try to make people see,
There is someone on high watching down,
Maybe in some ways I was chosen,
To bear a curse most do not know,
That redemption may come to someone like me.

Other Malevolents

If I exist,
Do you not realize that others do?
There is so much wrong in this world,
The approach of night,
Ever creeping, ever encroaching,
It scares some of us to the core,
Chills the blood of an already cold,
Stone weary heart.
Beasts of darkness exist before you,
There are so many ignorant ones,
Monsters are often internalized,
Instead of externalized.
We refuse to believe in real monsters,
While I exist in this world.
Many of these things are older,
More ancient,
More powerful,
Then even I.
I once thought I was a lonely evil,
Until I saw the evil of the ages,
Demonic forces, Satanic foes,
They exist and we often deny it,
We try to rationalize the reality,
Instead of accepting it.
We think there is a meaning,
When there might not be,
There is not always reason to the evil in this world,
There is no reason for me.

The Wolf

In the shadows,
The ever-present darkness,
I hunt.
Pacing around in the fresh snow,
Sniffing the scent of mortal flesh,
The hunger rumbling the stomach.
I see my prey,
Innocent, inattentive,
As they walk down the path,
Of self-righteousness.
Do I show them who they are?
Put them in their place,
So they can see where the real strength lies,
In my ancient blood,
In my ancient bones.
I can smell the iron in your blood,
Hear the drum beat of your heart,
As you anticipate the coming,
Await the beast within.
I can see in the dark,
Like it was pure sunlight to you,
Nothing the shadows conceal,
Is hidden to me.
Even if I could not see in the dark,
I could smell your blood,
Smell the hunger,
Smell the fear,
That you hold within you.
Yet I approach,
Try to run,
Try to escape,
I love the chase.

Hidden Thoughts

You try to hide what you think,
But I can hear your song,
It rings like music,
Like a dirge in my mind.
You cry in panic,
When I show you my true face,
The monster within,
Feeds off the fear you try to hide.
The thoughts of your terror,
Feed my desire.
You think I cannot hear you,
You think I cannot feel your fear,
But it is there,
The sweet song,
The wine of music.
I brought you here to hear this song,
The silk of the night bares all,
To the shadow,
To the ever night.
If I could share my thoughts with you,
You would tremble with more fear,
With preternatural terror,
Unlike any you have known.
Yet within your thoughts,
I hear hope,
Love.
My fears now increase,
As I consider the monster within,
And how I am about to feed.

Cult of the Shade

It is sad really,
The cults that worship my kind,
Like I am some kind of deity,
To be revered for my power.
I was mortal once too,
Though I died,
There was a time I bled,
Like them,
Like you.
They are foolish,
To think their worship,
Will appease me,
Into making them Shades.
Residents of Sheol like me.
They make for easy hunting,
If I care not for the chase,
Though they do not know my face,
I know each of theirs.
I have pursued them all,
Sought them out one by one,
Stopped them from hurting the innocent,
In savage sacrifices to my name.
They claim to know me,
But they know nothing,
The cold is not what they desire,
My blood is not for them,
This is not a gift,
Even though they praise me for it.

Immortal Insanity

Is this immortality really a gift?
Many have fallen along the way,
Victims not just of the inquisitors,
But of their own minds.
The long ages seem like a gift,
But the strongest will can crumble,
Under the weight of the ages.
Some have seen madness as something good,
But when the undead are mad,
The blood flows like floods,
Like rivers of gore.
They care not about rules of ours,
Laws that are in place for thousands of years,
We made them to protect ourselves,
To ensure our survival.
But monsters give in to their beast,
They rage against the culture,
The stability of the world,
Something I have tried to maintain.
Black tides may come,
Red rage will consume the will,
Not all are strong enough,
To resist the coming storm.

Sounds of the City

I stand above the din of the city,
Aware, listening,
To every cry and laugh,
To every song and fight.
Yet I still can hear your voice,
Echoing in the streets,
The song of your words,
Ringing in the wind.
The city cannot drown out the melody,
It is too strong,
I am weak before it,
As it resonates in my bones.
While people are born,
While people die,
Iron chariots crash and burn,
Buildings fall and arise,
There is that song,
Your voice,
Coming above the roofs to my home.
Like a choir of angels,
Singing to the shepherds of Bethlehem,
Your voice comes to me.
It soothes me,
Calms the blood beast within,
Makes the desire to feed,
Quiet to nothing more than a purr.
The sounds of the city,
Cannot drown you out,
I hear you when I rise,
And in the morning when I rest.

Burning Light

The sun scorches my skin,
I cannot take the natural light,
Of the ruler of the day,
The warmer and light of life.
None of my children can,
They all suffer from this curse,
This dreadful seed,
That drains us of colour and hope.
We miss the sunlight,
It gave us hope when we lived,
And now as we are dead,
The moon is our only hope.
But it is dead,
Reflected light,
That does not carry the warmth,
The warmth we so desire.
To see the flowers again,
In full sunlight,
Colours abounding in full bloom,
Is a gift you will never understand.
We only see things in shades,
In shadows,
Of what they are meant to be.
Do not take for granted,
The light that shines each day,
If it would not send me back to Sheol,
I would enjoy its warmth,
Its hope, each day.
Rise and shine in the sunlight,
For us, it is nothing but burning light.

Fog at Midnight

The clouds come down,
To collect their dew,
As tax collectors of old,
Pillaging the poor and meek.
I move in the mists,
Unseen,
Unheard,
To find you in the dark.
You sleep in the fog,
Tucked under your bed,
Warm and confident in your rest.
I wait outside until your dreams come,
Then become one with the fog,
To enter a forbidden place.
You do not know I am there,
I watch while you dream.
I cannot dream you see,
It is a gift of a mortal mind.
I try to imagine what it is like,
But I am a fog in the wind,
Gently caressing the moon,
Where you can never be.
I descend to your window,
But I dare not enter,
I am the abomination,
Not of this natural world.
So I go from this place,
Drift with the fog to some place new,
Where I can be what I am,
What I have become.

Mortal Hunters

Foolishness,
Some mortals try to hunt us,
To exterminate our kind,
From the face of their precious earth.
We are too old,
Too strong,
To be stamped out so easily.
Their convictions carry them,
Believing in old tales,
That carry no weight in reality.
They bear crosses thinking we fear them,
But they have no effect on us,
They do not burn or repel us,
It is a child's legend.
Yet they hunt.
Diligently they seek us,
To flush us out like waste,
Thinking us as lesser creatures,
Nothing but animals to be put to sleep.
We are immortals,
Created by powers they never understand.
We would not be here,
If our existence meant nothing.
We are the other side of the balance,
Bring us all down,
There will be consequences.
Yet they hunt us,
They kill us,
With foolish hopes.

Judgment Comes

I have been too long,
Separated from my own kind,
Enraptured by your light,
By the beauty of your grace.
I have stood,
Judging the world,
For sins you cannot comprehend,
For sins I have committed.
I have judged lesser Shades,
For crimes that would endanger us,
But cared nothing for mortal flesh.
Now I sit here,
In danger for things I have done,
To my own kind,
To protect you from their evil.
They tried to kill you,
To take you away from the light,
Not to make you one of us,
Just to force me to watch you die,
So that I would come back to the fold.
I found their hunters,
And brought them to a heavenly justice,
Yet more will come,
More will find us,
You stand in the halls of their fury,
Because I have dared to love you,
Because you dared to touch me,
In a way no one else has.

Moonfaced

I have never seen you in the day,
I simply cannot ever do that,
Yet even in the light of the moon,
I see innocence and beauty.
My cold flesh may never warm you,
The rays of the silver night,
Reaching down to comfort even me,
Though the light will never reveal you.
Your face is light enough,
It makes my dead heart believe,
Believe in something I have forgotten,
When my breath was stolen from me.
Smile, not just for you,
But for me as well,
As there is light enough in that for both.
Though I am not ashamed of what I am,
I cannot believe you would accept me,
For the pain I have caused in ages past,
When the moon was not so bright.
It never beamed so brightly as it does,
In the moment stuck in time,
When you look into my eyes,
To say what I hope to hear.
The silver light is my refuge,
While it brings out your eyes,
There is fire there still,
For us both to survive.

Crypt Sleeper

Many of us sleep in despair,
Dank dirty holes,
Meant for none but the mortal dead.
Stone effigies set up,
To honour the ones that passed,
Where some Shades sleep,
Resting, passing the day away.
The dead do not matter to us,
They are a reminder of who we are,
Yet defile these tombs,
These crypts built by human hands,
So that we may sleep in peace,
In a place where we find security.
The reason some fear the graveyard,
Is because of these crypt sleepers,
They arise and feed on those in the yard,
Paying respects to honoured dead.
We do not care,
Who you honour,
Who you come to acclaim.
You are cattle to us,
And the bones of these oxen,
Are a blanket we wrap ourselves in,
To find surety in sleep.
No one will open a crypt,
Open a mausoleum in the day,
Except to bury one of their newly dead.
We know the schedules,
When the newly dead are coming.
You will not find us,
There are many crypts to hide in,
Many crypts in which to never be found.

The Roamer

There was a time,
I wandered many empty streets,
Looking for something I did not expect,
Or even know I was looking for.
I filled up on blood,
On mortal terrors,
To feed my hungry beast,
But none satisfied,
None quenched the need to kill.
Around the globe I roamed,
London, Paris, Rome, New York,
But all these places were the same.
Wanting mortals,
To fragile to be mindful,
Of things that roam the night.
Though I found them beautiful,
They were as empty as me inside,
If not emptier,
More hollow,
More sullen.
So, I continued to go about,
Seeking for a truth I did not know,
Not knowing where I would find it.
The stats themselves could not answer me,
In all their ageless wisdom.
I have come now to this place,
To finally call it my home,
For there is something here,
Calling me,
And I cannot leave it.

A Pit of Sheol

Some have asked for a tale,
Of what Sheol was like,
Yet I fear to tread back to that place,
Even in my memories.
When I awoke in the land of the dead,
I was in a pit,
Held fast by two creatures,
With claws for hands,
And bone wings on their backs.
They were age old Shades,
Ones who have gone before me,
And they stabbed me with bone spears,
Over and over,
Even past the point I could bear.
They would burn my dead skin,
With hellfire from the deepest pits of despair,
Making me scream in their delight.
Within this pit I was confronted,
With every desire of mortal flesh,
But turned into a nightmare.
Though it seemed it would save me,
It really condemned me,
Made me hate the world and everything around me.
There was no escape,
No telling when the torture would end.
I did escape,
To a door unseen,
Not remembered,
How I found it, I do not know,
But it was a salvation,
Even if it led to the deathless state.

Eternal Curse

If I could lift this curse from me,
I am not sure I would.
True I miss the sunlight,
The smell of roses,
The scent of the trees in the wind.
Some have tried to separate themselves,
From the curse they have been given,
Yet there is no cure,
No power on earth to lift it,
Yet they try.
Even I, the first of us,
Cannot lift that state,
The cold and eternal death.
If anyone is capable of doing this,
It is Yahweh alone,
Yet I have never seen it done,
What grace can be given to do so?
Is this the thorn we all must bear?
Unfortunately, it is so.
Even when I asked the messiah,
The one sent to save all people,
He did not answer me,
Simply to say to rely on the grace,
Given to all people,
Even including the Shades.

Assassins

There are some that know of us,
Though we try to remain unknown.
Powerful men of church and state,
That use us for their own gain.
They crave power,
Nothing but the corruption it brings,
And some of the Shades have given into it,
They hire themselves out,
To hunt for blood for mortal gain,
To make a living in a merciless world.
They kill, not for sport,
Like the rest of us,
But for material gain.
They cannot be stopped by mortal means,
Making them deadly to their quarry.
Lightning fast,
As strong as thunder,
They move in shadows.
Reeking having wherever they go.
I have judged many for their carelessness,
For getting to close to exposing us.
They are a danger to living and dead alike,
But their worries are small and meaningless.
Some have tried to hunt me down,
Not realizing who I am,
They have all been sent back to their own,
Unsuccessful, weak and pathetic.

Mortal Evil

I am a breed of evil,
I cannot help it,
The beast inside me wants to eat and destroy,
Not withhold from the hunt.
Humanity, what is its reason?
It eliminates entire towns,
Nations,
Races,
For what?
What root causes such evil?
Has the devil been reborn in mortal flesh?
They look at us as a breed to exterminate,
Without looking at themselves.
Humans hate, kill, destroy,
Manipulate, con, deceive.
True, we do some of these things,
It's in our beastial nature.
Humans have a choice,
They were made good,
Though fallen,
They still have a choice to make.
Does that make them better than us?
Or worse?
They cannot justify the evils they cause,
All for self-ambition,
I have seen the destruction of their own sins,
While condemning us for ours.
Look in the mirror oh human race,
Pull the plank out of your own eye,
Before burning us in the daylight.

The Meeting Point

So, where do we meet at?
I, the monster,
You, the beautiful one.
Can I think that you would be,
The one to cure my deathless state?
I find no peace,
In anything in this world,
Yet you give me something,
Something I do not understand.
When I think of what I can offer you,
I come up empty.
I do not want you to suffer for eternity,
I exist in turmoil,
I would save you from that.
There is a place I think I could understand,
That you would take me in,
But I must find the cure first,
Though there is none.
The point that we meet,
Is that we both desire the same thing,
To feel alive,
But you are the one that lives,
I could never be that again.
Even if I were to live again,
I do not know how to do life,
It is unfathomable to me,
Yet there is something in your eyes,
That makes it possible.

Nothing Left for Us

I cannot do this,
I do not deny that I need you,
That my eternity would be less punishable,
Less wearisome
With you around.
Yet I cannot give you the kiss of death,
The passionate embrace that you desire.
I think there is too much left for you,
To do in your short life,
To take away what you could become.
There is no guarantee,
That you would not be a monster,
After I made you like me,
I could not bear to have to judge you,
To have to send you to eternal death.
You give me such hope,
So much belief,
That this world is a better place.
I left a world of evil and darkness,
To see you in the light,
But there is nothing on this side,
That could contain you.
You are the grace that is given this world,
I could not take it away,
Do not ask me to make you like me,
I feel that it is time,
To send you to your life,
To your true destiny.

Lord of the Dead

I have lived for ages past,
Since before the flood,
Before written history.
Always I have commanded the Shades,
The dead things long forgotten.
Though many of these children,
Have forgotten their progenitor,
The reason they have unlife.
I am spoken of in myths,
In riddles long foretold,
Yet none know my name.
I can feel them all around the world,
Killing, thrashing,
Making this world their hell.
But all will come to end,
When I stand up to bring them down,
Judgment will come,
I will see it made whole.
Only I have the power to unite,
Or unbind,
The trapped souls in endless death.
I sit on a throne of bone,
Overseeing their unholy tests,
Trying to prove their despicable worth.
I hold the keys to their salvation,
Do they not see where they are headed?
It is time for me to show myself,
For I am Azrael,
The vengeance angel,
I am, the Lord of the Dead.

www.ingramcontent.com/pod-product-compliance
Lightning Source LLC
Chambersburg PA
CBHW042112100526
44587CB00025B/4022